SATORI

AWAKENING

We dedicate this book to the ancient sages,
to all seekers of Truth and to those
who have just begun their journey.

Satguru Shri Mahayogi Paramahansa

SATORI
AWAKENING

Words of Truth from
Satguru Shri Mahayogi Paramahansa

Edited by

MAHAYOGI YOGA MISSION
New York

SATORI
AWAKENING
Words of Truth from Satguru Shri Mahayogi Paramahansa
Copyright © 2010 MAHAYOGI YOGA MISSION

For information:
MAHAYOGI YOGA MISSION
228 Bleecker St., #12
New York, NY, 10014
www.mahayogiyogamission.org

Library of Congress Catalog Card Number: 2010932537
ISBN: 978-0-9663555-2-9

Contents

~ Acknowledgements ~

*First and foremost, we offer our highest veneration
and deepest gratitude to our*

Honorable Master,
Satguru Shri Mahayogi Paramahansa,

*for the priceless gift of this book. We gratefully
acknowledge our Master's dedicated guidance
throughout the entire publishing process, including
project planning, editing and design.*

We express our sincere gratitude to Anandamali,
Director of Mahayogi Yoga Mission in New York, for her
devotion, selfless work and unending commitment to Satori,
and for faithfully documenting and translating the Master's
precious teachings. We thank the following disciples:
Sanatana, for sharing his expertise in Sanskrit, his devotion
and endless energy in creating the preface and glossary;
Gauranga and Niranjan, for editing; Karuna from the Atman
design team, for layout and design production; Yoshichika
Murakami, for photo editing; and the many brothers and
sisters of Mahayogi Yoga Mission who contributed to this book
by documenting, editing, proofreading, or in any other form.

Om Tat Sat, Om

Preface

Satori, or Awakening, is a simple word, but it has a profound and enthralling meaning. It is an entrance to an unknown world and, at the same time, to our own source, which should be more familiar than anything. This book is actually the doorway to Awakening. Satguru Shri Mahayogi Paramahansa simply teaches Awakening, and the most direct way to it. You may ask, "If I should awaken to something, to what do I awaken and what then is the world that I am perceiving now?" You may also wonder if there really is a way to Awakening. The answer to these questions is what Shri Mahayogi teaches.

His guidance is delivered at *satsanghas*, sacred gatherings among seekers of Truth. Traditionally in India, this is the form in which people are given the opportunity to be in the presence of an enlightened being and receive his or her teachings. This tradition cannot be handed down superficially—it requires a living master at its center, a *guru* who has realized the Truth and embodies it in every sense. Such a living master, or enlightened being, is one who can actually guide you to Awakening.

The presence of Shri Mahayogi, a Master who lives in this age, has inevitably drawn people who, consciously or unconsciously, are seeking the truth of their own self or of this world. The words of Truth that flow from his mouth have inspired many to earnestly seek to awaken to the Truth—the True Self. The teachings of Yoga, as confirmed by the Master's direct experience, lead seekers to remove their obstacles to Awakening: the mind's ignorance of the Truth, egoism, and all other attachments. His clear explanations guide each individual to a direct understanding of Truth, Reality, and the non-Truth that covers the True Self.

Shri Mahayogi always dispenses a teaching in direct response to the inner condition, personal circumstance and level of understanding of the individual facing him, most often in answer to a particular question. People of many different nationalities and ages have asked diverse questions, and all have received meaningful answers. Shri Mahayogi teaches the practice of Yoga as the most certain and concrete method to the realization of the Truth, the True Self, also called God.

Yoga has been passed on and developed in India since ancient times. However, it is not limited to a particular place and time. Shri Mahayogi's appearance in the modern day, in a different country is a clear indication of the universality of the Truth, and of Yoga as the way to its attainment. Yoga can be understood and experienced by anyone, regardless of condition or circumstance.

Merely sitting before Shri Mahayogi and looking into his compassionate eyes brings indescribable peace. Not only the seeker of Truth, but anyone who suffers, feels as though he or she has come home after a long journey. This proves that Satori is not an intellectual achievement, but the original state of humanity as a whole.

The Master's natural Awakening at the age of eight confirms that there is no need for a particular background or tradition in order to attain Enlightenment. The Truth is simple and universal. It is the essence of all human beings, and of all that is animate and inanimate. Shri Mahayogi manifests this Truth as Supreme Love. The love of God, or Truth—the essence of everything—is what the Master's existence reveals to us.

Satori collects the teachings of Satguru Shri Mahayogi Paramahansa, as given to visitors and disciples during *satsanghas* in Kyoto, Osaka, and New York, from May 2000 to February 2006. These conversations will bring you directly to the truth about the goal of your life, the essence of yourself, the reality of the world, and the path to Awakening. Think them over. To do so is already the practice of Yoga. We hope you meditate on the Truth and feel the vast existence of Shri Mahayogi himself, which fully expresses the reality of your own Self.

SANATANA

Mahayogi Yoga Mission
16 August 2010

Introduction

At age eight, Satguru Shri Mahayogi Paramahansa spontaneously entered *Nirvikalpa Samadhi*, complete absorption into the True Consciousness without any notion or concept, and realized the *Atman*—the True Self. He awoke to Non-dual Reality.

In his later adolescence, he underwent the intensive practice of Yoga, which was virtually unknown in Japan at that time. He soon mastered the most austere *asanas* (yogic postures). Then, through meditation, he distinctly and thoroughly unveiled the underlying structure and the actual nature of the body, the mind, and the universe. Solely by his own direct experience, without relying on anything external, he realized the essence of Yoga and mastered all its branches, proving that they are all genuine paths for Awakening to Divine Reality—Enlightenment.

As bees naturally gather around the nectar of the lotus flower, seekers were drawn to the divine light of Shri Mahayogi, and sought his guidance. In 1976, his followers established the Mahayogi Yoga Ashrama at his home in Kyoto, Japan—the site of his complete Awakening. Since then, many have visited the ashrama and received the teachings of Truth.

Shri Mahayogi is permanently established in the complete bliss of final liberation. He guides each person according to his or her individual disposition, character and need. He teaches the exceedingly complex and subtle aspects of Yoga, as well as their application in everyday life, in a way that anyone can easily comprehend. Many who have experienced his peerless wisdom and deep compassion have found a perfect entry into Truth.

In 1996, through the invitation of two disciples, Shri Mahayogi visited New York, where seekers became enthralled with the Master, who shone with the light of Truth. Mahayogi Yoga Mission was then established in New York that same year. Disciples began to intensify their practice and disseminate his teachings. Shri Mahayogi now travels between Kyoto and New York, and has visited other countries. He continues to guide seekers in the most appropriate and direct way, thus enabling them to realize through their own experience, the primordial True Self— beyond name, gender, race, nationality and religion.

Mahayogi Yoga Mission
Publications Team
August, 2010

NOTE: Brackets enclose editorial interpolations to clarify or explain surrounding text.

SATORI
AWAKENING

Words of Truth from
Satguru Shri Mahayogi Paramahansa

I

Auspiciousness

(On the occasion of the Master's Jayanti *
Sunday, 23 November 2003, Kyoto)*

The Value of Life

There is a saying, "Everything is suffering." The basis of this saying is that if death is the ultimate suffering, then aging, sickness and, primordially, having a body of flesh—even birth itself—are all nothing but causes of suffering. From this point of view, a birthday may be so repugnant as to leave no reason to celebrate. This is just one point of view.

Granted, this is true from the perspective of the interwoven world of mind and body. But by renouncing this ever-changing world, mind and body, by finding and realizing the Truth, everything is transformed into bliss. It is only because you were born that you can realize and experience this. That is why being born into flesh becomes an auspicious and blessed occasion.

Since ancient times, sages have taught that the human soul, the human life, is invaluable and precious, because it enables us to seek and realize the Truth. Truly, the event of birth into a human body is fundamentally auspicious. You will come to know that the perception of seeing everything as suffering is an error of the mind.

Truth is eternally unchangeable. It will not "one day" appear. Truth has existed, it still exists now, and will exist forever. Truth can never change nor break, let alone perish. Each of you, rejoice in your birth, in the fact that you were born as a human being who can possibly realize the Truth, and make this birth auspicious.

4

True Self

(Saturday, 27 May 2000, Kyoto)

Today, the sound of heavy, pouring rain resonates throughout the ashrama*. *In addition to the regular members, several visitors from the asana and meditation class are in attendance, including Nagaishi from Osaka. The* satsangha* *begins with everyone amiably looking over an original image of the cover design of* The Universal Gospel of Yoga*, *the English version of which Mahayogi Yoga Mission is presently hard at work to complete. An attendee asks Shri* Mahayogi* about the contents of the book. The* ashrama *is brought into great stillness. Only the sound of falling rain can be heard.*

Existence, Consciousness and Supreme Bliss

Master: Truth is unchanging. It has been expressed through various words in different countries throughout the ages. India, especially, has a great tradition of this, and has maintained an abundant compilation of sacred scriptures, collectively called the Vedas*. For thousands of years before writing existed, the Vedas were passed down orally from master to disciple. As time went on, and writing was invented, the Vedas were then recorded. These writings are what we now know as sacred scriptures.

As we read these classical scriptures, we see that humanity's hopes, anxieties and thoughts have always been commonly shared, regardless of differences in time, place, culture and customs. Within this tradition, there were many questions and answers to a variety of topics, that led to the ultimate question: "**What is the truth of this world and of our existence?**" Of course, the word "God" has existed from time immemorial, and so has the sense of awe and the act of divine prayer. Yet, it appears that there were also people in the past who must have searched with great sincerity for the answer to "What is God?," and [pondered], "If God exists, we must be able to perceive God; furthermore, we must be able to have direct contact with God." With this conviction, they proceeded to devote themselves entirely to meditation and self-discipline.

Now, what is this Reality that is described as **Existence?** We usually identify the objects perceived through our sense organs as existence. For example, let's say there is a cup here; it exists. But the form of this cup was different in the past, and it may smash into small pieces and cease to exist in the future. This means that this cup is neither absolute nor eternal. So, referring to the word "existence" or "reality," what is truly eternal? Just like the cup, our body is the same. One day a body is born, then it grows larger into a man or woman, or an animal or plant; it takes various forms, and then eventually it is gone. It is the same with the mind. When we are children, our minds are filled with various thoughts, and as we mature, our minds fill with different thoughts. At each respective moment, these thoughts are a reality for the mind. But this reality is ever-changing; therefore, it is not permanent. We think it exists, but it can never be Absolute Existence.

In life experiences, there are happy times and, likewise, unhappy times. There are joyful periods and painful periods. However, none of these conditions are permanent. If there is something unchangeable that exists within these changeable circumstances, it must have infinite value. This is what is called "God," Truth or the True Consciousness of "I." This also is uncertain until we confirm its veracity. The word "God" or "God-as-Existence" is not something established by a religion; God does not depend upon religions, philosophies, words or anything else. It stands alone. It exists by itself. If this were not the case, God would be subservient to a certain religion. Truth is beyond all, and yet, it is the foundation of the whole of creation. It is eternal, **imperishable Existence**. The mind, however, does not know this.

Naturally, when we speak about our own experiences or thoughts we use the word "I" for the first person. The protagonist says, "I think," "I feel," and so on. But no one really knows what this "I" really signifies. No one knows the true "I." If you feel that your "I" is happy, it would have to be permanently so; no pain, sadness or worry should arise because that would contradict this happiness. However, your "I" often experiences the depths of suffering the very next day after your "I" once proclaimed its happiness. If your "I" keeps changing, then the question naturally arises: just what is this "I"?

Objective analysis leads to the following example: if you lose your arm, you do not lose a part of yourself, do you? Your "I" still exists as "I." What is injured or lost is only a part of the body. If you cannot hear, see or speak, your "I" still exists, the same as everyone else. Is this not so? So the first person "I-consciousness" has nothing to do with your physical shortcomings or health.

It is the same with the mind. The sense of happiness or despair, that which satisfies the mind or pulls it into darkness—all such experience—belongs to the mind. The mind regards these experiences as a part of the world. So, to speak accurately, it is "my mind" that is happy or "my mind" that suffers. Usually your "I" is entangled with the experiences of the mind, which is how you feel happy, unhappy, joyful, sad, angry or compassionate, continually changing and tossed about as circumstances or events continue to change.

This is the Truth, of the utmost urgency to learn and to know: what really is this "I"? Well, "I" is changeless. Regardless of the body's conditions, or how the world is, or even the mind's reactions, "I" is the Consciousness that simply knows and sees them. Needless to say, it is not ego-consciousness. Ego-consciousness is self-centered consciousness; it is that which separates itself from others. It belongs to the mind; it is a major component of the mind's foundation. The True Self is the consciousness that exists further within, and knows all the other states of the mind.

It is really a strange phenomenon. Since all of you are conscious of your "I," it's impossible that you don't know who you truly are. But if you can palpably distinguish the **Consciousness** of the **True Self** from your own mind, and realize that they are different, all your confusions and worries will be resolved. What you must learn is this "I." The concrete way to realize this is meditation. In order to make yourself ready for meditation, you need to train and prepare the body and the breath.

Visitor: I admit that it is a bit difficult to understand. Something exists besides the mind?

Master: Right now, you know that you are thinking about something, don't you? Objectively, you can grasp that you are thinking about something, right? This Consciousness, which grasps or knows what you are thinking now, is always there, without change. The mind is constantly thinking about many things. Sometimes, the mind is not aware of anything, as in deep sleep, but right now you can understand all of your mind's thoughts or feelings, right? That Consciousness is It.

(Shri Mahayogi gives darshan* *to each attendee. The sound of falling rain bathes the silence.)*

Chetaka: In the book, *A Search in Secret India*, by Paul Brunton, there is a part in which Ramana Maharshi* states that from the fact that all human beings are ever wanting happiness untainted with sorrow, and from the fact that they love themselves most, our search for happiness is an unconscious search for our True Self. Thinking about it, I wonder: Does the motivation to act upon our desires or upon our inclinations for self-preservation imply that we are seeking the True Self?

Master: Yes. Everything in this world—not just humans, but animals, plants and other beings, this whole universe—seeks its own happiness. Although they go through struggles for existence and natural selection, as well as the arising of many conflicts and problems, without question, there lies the principle of the pursuit of happiness. The great difference is in the quest for selfish happiness or selfless happiness. It is only because so many insist upon their own happiness that the destruction of the happiness of others results, as has happened often throughout the history of the world—even in the name of religion. To fulfill the desire for self-benefit, or one's own sole happiness, people have conquered and even enslaved others.

The motivation to seek or pursue happiness is in everyone. If you ask thieves, they may insist that they feel happiness in thieving. If you ask police officers or judges, they may say that their happiness is in catching criminals and bringing them to justice. All other people have their various claims to happiness as well. So, unless you go a step further, and until you find the answer to universal happiness or absolute happiness, personal happiness cannot be Truth. When we say "happiness" it suggests an eternal, unchanging and universal happiness, and the fact that people desire happiness shows that there is an inherent sense of happiness that is true and lasting.

In the *Vedanta** philosophy of India, the words *Sat-Chit-Ananda** express the Truth. *Sat* is **Existence** or Reality, which is permanent and absolute—it neither changes nor disappears. *Chit* is the **Consciousness** that knows that, and *Ananda** is **Supreme Bliss** or Happiness. Our essence is the Truth, or *Sat-Chit-Ananda*. But when the mind is veiled by ignorance it forgets the Truth, bringing false ideas, and *Sat-Chit-Ananda* comes to be reflected in a selfish way.

Why do we pursue happiness in this world? Why do we desire happiness to be everlasting? Why do we want to feel happiness, enjoy it to the fullest and revel in this happiness? It is just a reflection of the Truth of our own existence, which is itself pure and eternal bliss. However, simply due to ignorance, we are in error. Since the world is ever-changing, there is nothing that exists permanently. It is now known that this universe, including entire galaxies, is constantly changing. Everything—even the tiniest particles of dust and the cells of living beings—is constantly changing, and nothing stays the same. The desire for "perfect" happiness in this world is like a sand castle. Sorrow and suffering are the inevitable result.

Chetaka: I read the parable of the musk deer in a book. The musk deer goes mad looking for the origin of a magical fragrance and eventually dies without finding it, not knowing all the while that the origin of this fragrance was on its own body. So, this story is also an example of searching for the Truth in the phenomena of the world.

Master: Yes, it is. There is a passage from an old sacred scripture expressing this in a much simpler manner: God created nine openings in the human body and arranged them to face outwards. Consequently, human beings are prevented from seeing inwards. So, they look only to the external world and do not realize that true happiness is within. These nine openings are the eyes, ears, nostrils, mouth, reproductive organs and excretory organs. The story of the musk deer relates the same principle. True happiness exists within the depth of our own minds, which is why the search for happiness in the external world alone is a false idea and a delusion. Even so, you should not be nihilistic and view this world as a false idea or a dream. This is also a mistaken view because, although the physical world is impermanent and constantly changes shape and form, our essence, as well as the essence of the universe, is the same: **True Existence**. The whole of creation is the

Beloved and the most highly cherished. (*The Master looks at another visitor.*) Do you understand? This is a very important point: do not become nihilistic. Quite simply, by the thorough and correct understanding of the Truth, you will also be able to correctly understand the world.

Chetaka: When one first becomes acquainted with Yoga and starts practicing *asanas**, after a few months of regular practice one may experience the condition of *shanti**, or contentment and calmness. And as one progresses, at least after studying with Shri Mahayogi for a few years, one may experience the unconditional joy that exists within. Is it a correct understanding to view this as a glimpse of the True Essence?

Master: Yes. The word "*Satori**" has existed since ancient times, and its meaning is [the realization of] the Truth. Because the Truth is everyone's essence and exists within all already, it is not something that someone can give to you or something that you can obtain. It emerges from within your own self. It exists as the essence, yet something prevents you from knowing it in the same way that clouds or fog hide the moon. This is caused by the mind. The mind is imperfect; it is neither omnipotent nor omniscient, which is why the mind must study and learn the Truth. By being taught, the mind will stop preventing you from knowing the Truth, and true happiness, or bliss, will emerge from within your own self. The state of the clouds covering the moon will then end, and a state free of suffering is realized.

The desire for or the feeling of "I want to know this or that" or "I want to obtain this or that" is all creation of the mind. Pure Consciousness has nothing to do with this, because it is in itself complete. To state it even more simply, it is the only Reality. It is the only thing unchanging and eternal. It is our very essence. The great Existence, which has been named "God," is That. The word "God" is only a term. God is **Eternal Existence**.

Freedom and Love

(Questions regarding the application of certain Yoga practices continue. Shri Mahayogi speaks to a guest who has just begun attending asana and meditation classes.)

Master: The study of Yoga is fascinating. It is much more interesting than any kind of schoolwork. You will enjoy the feeling of knowing that you have begun to discover what the universe is, and of having found an answer to such mysteries of the world.

Everyone desires freedom as much as they desire happiness. However, this world has many limitations. When day comes, night follows. Night is then surely overcome by day. The body or the mind can taste temporary freedom, and then, soon after, feels non-freedom. Because of your attachment to certain conditions you consequently feel non-freedom. However, the soul, as the substance or essence, is inherently happy and free. There is no non-freedom at all. Because the ego or the selfish "I" and its attachments—the desire to possess happiness, freedom, or whatever—cannot be fulfilled in this world after all, you then experience non-freedom. Therefore, if the selfish "I" and the sense of "mine" are removed, you will be free, since no longer can anything remain attached.

Attachments are just like holding something with your hand (*gesturing as if to grasp something with each hand*). When you hold on to this and that (*showing both hands grasping*), this state is not free. If you let go (*releasing his hands*), you are free; you can grasp and release again freely (*closing and opening his hands*) It is perfect freedom! If you can handle circumstances and situations in your life like this, you will be released from the sense of bondage. You can remain detached, no matter what comes to you— be it something good or something bad.

(*Shri Mahayogi laughs briskly and continues.*)

The idea of "love"—considered ever more important today—is the same. What is love? Love is the same principle as freedom. The lover, the beloved and love itself—if you are attached to any one of them, suffering is sure to come in abundance. You all may have experienced the beginnings of a love relationship as being very pure. One is constantly giving of oneself. One strives to do whatever the loved one desires. But as time progresses that love may start to change form. It is wonderful if the love between two people is blessed to be true love; but often, changes in each person's mind cause the relationship to crumble. When this happens, one may try to enslave the other under the name of love, or the love may even turn to hatred.

The feeling of giving, which one possessed in the beginning, can change into forcing the other person to give. This is a common scenario with human love. If the love grows purely, one will always wish for the other's happiness. The true form of love is to make the other happy, rather than to make oneself happy. It is a wonderful experience to love another person—or to love anything—but you must be very careful not to love your "self" (ego) over another.

(Nagaishi first came to see Shri Mahayogi because she was moved by the books Pranava Sara* *and* The Universal Gospel of Yoga. *Quietly listening for some time, she begins her question.)*

Nagaishi: I heard that there was a *satsangha* every Saturday, so I attended one for the first time four months ago, and this is now my second one. I am so grateful. Thank you very much.

First, I would like to tell you what I was asked to convey by my friend who attended this first *satsangha* with me. He also met Shri Mahayogi for the first time that same day, and it has been four months since he returned to America. Interestingly, he said that Shri Mahayogi is in his heart all the time. Thank you very much.

Master (smiling): Is it so? That is a good report.

Nagaishi: And when I told him that Shri Mahayogi would be in New York sometime soon, he said that he would like to visit you there sometime within the three months of your stay. (*Shri Mahayogi nods deeply.*)

I do not study or practice Yoga, but when we met you, I asked you, "Please tell us what we should do when we return to the mundane world," and you answered, "Exert yourselves to service completely." This has been really helpful for me the past four months, as if a battery was fully recharged. Now, each time I need to make a judgment about something, I have been trying to discriminate in every moment whether there is Truth in it or not. Like my friend, Shri Mahayogi has been visiting my heart with those words. It has changed not only abstract aspects but also so much of my concrete situations. My position within my circumstances has also started to change a great deal, so I am really amazed.

(It seems that after Nagaishi visited Shri Mahayogi, so many changes have truly kept happening around her. She continues with a bit of light excitement.)

I was first introduced to you and your teachings through books, and I have been taught that there is an answer or a goal, even if it seems far away. I am so grateful for what I have been receiving through your words—and something deeper within—since my first meeting with you. Thank you very much.

Master: Thank you very much. Even though I will be away for a while, they will gather here regularly just like this. I will return soon.

A few days later, Shri Mahayogi left Japan. Many people in New York have been longing for the Master's blessing, and to taste universal love and Truth through him.

III

Eternal Truth

(Sunday, 31 March 2002, Osaka)

The day is warm, with a clear blue sky. This year spring arrives earlier than ever recorded. The disciples from Osaka had requested that Shri Mahayogi come to Osaka when the cherry blossoms bloom, and on March 31, 2002, he granted their wish. They are delighted to see Shri Mahayogi, who reciprocates with a full smile.

The disciples in Osaka have been practicing earnestly and devotedly. Since the class began the autumn before last, it has been progressing wonderfully. Today, the seriousness and the one-pointed concentration of the attendees creates an extraordinary spiritual mood. Their passion for Yoga continues to heighten swiftly. This enthusiasm makes possible the special blessing of the Master's visit for satsangha *in Osaka.*

Daily Practice and Meditation

Satsangha *begins as soon as Shri Mahayogi takes a seat.*

Suddenly, heavy drops of rain, as in a tropical storm, fall from what was a pristine sky. This little surprise puts everyone's slightly nervous mind at ease. In this joyful and light atmosphere, Takagi, though a bit hesitant, begins to speak. She has been diligently attending classes since the end of last year.

Takagi: Well...I would like to have your guidance on how to practice meditation.

Master: Before answering your question, you must understand that there are three necessities for daily Yoga practice.

First is discipline, or training using the physical body. This is, for all of you, *asana* and *pranayama**.

Secondly, cultivate your understanding of the Truth. Concretely, this includes studying the right scriptures, reflecting on the words of Truth, and cultivating the correct understanding.

Lastly, deepen your aspiration for, or contemplation of the divine—further, focus on divine Existence, as if you are deeply in love.

By practicing these three things daily, your practice becomes *kriya yoga**. "*Kriya*" means to "put into action."

Now, to return to your original question, the objects of meditation are also divided into three categories.

One is discrimination. You examine whether your everyday thoughts and activities are based on the Truth or not; whether there are any contradictions. By studying sacred scriptures and listening to the right words of Truth, you will develop the ability to discriminate whether or not your thoughts are correct.

Another one is self-inquiry—the meditation to seek out the Self, of which all of you must be aware, but perhaps not certain—what the True Self is, what your own Self is. Usually, you identify your self with your experiences, social position, abilities, mind, body, or things you have learned through social conditioning. However, these are only temporary conditions that are built upon changing circumstances. Once you were a child and youthful, and in the future you will be old. Whether male or female, and regardless of age, "I-consciousness" must always be the same. However, people often identify the self with these changing conditions and forget the True Self. This leads to the experience of happiness and unhappiness toward their circumstances. The True Self is the Consciousness that simply knows and sees, neutrally and quite objectively, no matter how your circumstances may change. In this Consciousness there is no individuality, no personal or racial discrimination; this Consciousness is universal and singular. To know this True Self is one of the most significant goals of meditation.

The third one is to concentrate and meditate upon a completed being, such as God or a divine and sacred Existence. We all have a physical body and we see things using our physical eyes. Abstract ideas, philosophy and words of Truth can be hard to grasp and are therefore difficult to realize. But, if there is a complete being with a physical body, who walks the earth as we do, the object becomes easier for us to grasp. Even though this divine figure has a human form, he or she is, in essence, the Truth itself; he or she is the embodiment of perfect Existence, free of any blemish. You should view such a being as a concrete manifestation of divine Existence. You should intensely yearn for it and worship it. Perhaps the word love is closer in meaning than the word worship. Intensely love and grow close to it, as if to unite with it. If you do so, then you will penetrate into the perfect Truth of the divine being, and consequently all impurities will disappear.

You must practice in this manner. Your ideal object for meditation can be very personal. So find the object to which you are naturally drawn in love, and use that as your ideal form of God. It is called your *ishta** or chosen ideal.

Truth is One

Vishoka: The closer we come to your teachings the more we notice their similarity to the teachings of Shri Ramakrishna*, Vivekananda*, and Paramahansa* Yogananda*, who were all born in the 19th century. Yet, you are giving us these teachings fit for the modern age and the world in which we are now living. I would be grateful if you could speak on this similarity, as well as the unique characteristics of your own teachings.

Master: Well, from ancient times there has been a well-known phrase recorded in an Indian sacred scripture: "Truth is One; the wise call it various." Without a doubt, whether one is awakened or not, Truth is unchangeable and must always be the same. If both Buddha* and Christ reached the ultimate state, their realization must be exactly the same. If there were even a subtle difference, it would indicate that one of these realizations is not of the Truth. Even a child who has not learned anything must perceive Truth the same way. It is eternal and unchangeable; the One without a second. So people came to see that the important thing was how to realize this Truth in actuality.

Their inquiry led to a specialized method, a way for realization, the teachings of which, once formed, came to be called Yoga. The core of Yoga is meditation. Through this means, *yogis** realized the three objects of meditation mentioned earlier—by direct experience. It has been conveyed that Buddha, or Shakyamuni*, also attained his great Awakening through meditation [the same way as *yogis* did]. He too, is considered to be one who has attained Yoga.

About two thousand and some hundred years later, when people had nearly forgotten about Truth, great awakened ones appeared to remind them. In recent times, there was the great awakened one, Shri Ramakrishna of Kolkata, [previously called Calcutta], whom Vishoka just mentioned, and his disciple Swami Vivekananda, who brought forth the Truth to the entire world. In the 19th century, India was subject to British colonization. It was a turbulent time during which Western civilization was invading the East. In Japan, it was the end of the Edo period and of the Tokugawa shogunate, and the beginning of the Meiji era. It was the time which heralded contact and exchange between the West and the East. In the present 21st century, world communication is quite immediate, due to the development of airplanes and information technology, but all of these changes were just starting in the 19th century. So, of course, the meeting of West and East resulted in various cultural and religious conflicts. It seems that these conflicts have yet to be resolved.

After his realization of Yoga, Shri Ramakrishna experienced and realized the Truth of various religions besides the one into which he was born. At one time he abandoned Hinduism and Yoga. Learning directly from a missionary, he practiced Christianity and was able to realize its Truth. He did the same with Islam. Through his experiences, he realized that **"Truth is One."**

The seers, or awakened ones, simply call Truth by various names. Even in India, different sacred scriptures use different words to describe it—"God," "the Absolute Principle of the Universe," "True Self," or "Soul"—the difference is simply in philosophy and in the name used by each seer. He or she must see the same absolute Truth even through another path. The name is a mere symbol or word used to represent the substance; the name is not the essence. Truth itself does not need any name, be it the word "Truth" or "God." There is no way to describe it by mere words, but *it is*. And you can awaken to it—because it is your very essence. It is the essence of the universe, the essence of all creation; this Eternal Existence is the essence of you yourself. You should **awaken to it** and **know yourself**. This is the absolute and final stage of the entire practice of Yoga.

The Realization of True Reality

Visitor: What kind of sensation will one have when Awakening happens?

Master: This, too, can only be explained with a metaphor. Everyone wakes up in the morning, right? When it happens, you are aware that you have awakened. It is the same. (*Everyone laughs.*)

Visitor: So, it's so natural...

Master: Yes, it is. You become aware of yourself after you wake up, right? Then, you negate the sleep-world by saying it was a dream or creation. Just like this, when you awaken into the Truth, you will understand that the dream-world in sleep and the world in which you are now is one and the same dream.

Visitor: So all is one...

Master: Yes. Within this [Absolute] Consciousness, there are no forms at all—even your own self is without form. This is the only Consciousness, which actually exists. In essence, all of you are That. In the One Absolute Consciousness, there is no relativity at all. If I am to use an example, it is like suddenly waking up in a dark void. You may ask, what's so good about that? Ordinarily, you strive to see or feel the reality of things, whatever they may be. However, they break down in time, no matter how solid they seem. Everything is constantly changing—and nothing is everlasting. But True Reality is absolutely free of the possibility of change. And *it is the only Reality that exists.* When you awaken to Reality, you will come to understand that galaxies and even the entire universe are but an empty dream.

As I mentioned, this is absolute *Satori.* In the pre-stages, some various experiences can occur. These experiences contain traces of the relative world, so they are not absolute. For instance, there is the phrase "universal consciousness." As this phrase suggests, there is an experience in which one's own body and mind disappear, and one feels a unity with the consciousness of the universe or the great void, or feel as if one's whole being is penetrating into the consciousness of space. And also, there is an experience in which you may feel yourself in all, or you may feel something like one existence or one consciousness. There are countless experiences that can happen in meditation, but as I said earlier, you must keep practicing until you *completely* awaken into Truth. And you should not feel that the process toward this must be long, because the Truth [already] exists within you. If it did not, then you would not have a physical body, and you would not even have this temporal existence. Know that the fact that you exist here and now is the very proof that **Truth** or **Reality** exists. So, by sincerely and intently deepening your meditation, you will experience the Truth, and you will awaken to it.

The Universality of Yoga

Master (continuing): This is the framework or central teaching of Yoga, which has been conveyed for thousands of years in India. Many different particulars were added as time went on and a system or philosophy was established. However, as I said before, Shri Ramakrishna, who appeared in the 19th century, and is regarded in India as an incarnation of God, taught that these complications are unimportant. He said be simple and simply think of God and by doing so, God will take notice and come to you.

Those of you who have been to India may know that it has long been a very conservative country, including its religious practices. The *brahmins**, who practiced sacred rituals, exercised absolute authority as a sector of the social system. It is in this social climate that Shri Ramakrishna and *yogis* have appeared singularly, from "the wild unknown," to teach the Truth.

As I mentioned earlier, I think that the **oneness of Truth** in all different religions is the great legacy that Shri Ramakrishna left to the people of the 20th and 21st centuries, and beyond. It serves to harmonize all people and beings in the world. I have heard, in fact, that the death toll from conflicts under the name of religion is now the highest in human history—it's quite foolish. Yoga is usually not called a religion; it is quite different from dualistic or general religions. Yoga contains the essence of all religions. If you hold onto dualistic religions you can never acknowledge that the Truth is One. People of many religions often take the view that their religion is the best.

The Truth that was realized and revitalized by Shri Ramakrishna was brought to America and Europe by his disciple Vivekananda. Still, branches of their organization continue to expand throughout the world even now. In India, it is called Ramakrishna Mission*. Our organization is called Mahayogi Yoga Mission. We too are called by the name "Mission" and, as Vishoka mentioned, there are many similarities and commonalities between us. As I said, "Truth is One," so as a matter of course, our Truth is the same.

If I may particularly speak of unique differences, I was born as a Japanese person in Japan. When you look at the long history of Yoga, almost all those who propagated it were Indian. But Yoga is universal. Race, culture and the color of one's skin have nothing to do with it. The Truth is One. Therefore, any religion that one practices is fine, because everyone surely comes to realize the same Truth eventually. This was and is the profound message of Yoga. Perhaps I was born Japanese as one way to demonstrate this (*smiling*). Yoga is not exclusive to Indian people but can be realized by someone who is Japanese, American, European, African, Asian or anybody; it does not matter what color one's skin is or what one's religion is. I would urge you all to actually prove this statement.

Another significant characteristic is the re-introduction of correct *asana* practice, which Shri Ramakrishna himself also experienced, and although he completely mastered it, he did not teach it, saying that it was unnecessary. There is now a necessity to re-establish the correct way to practice *asana*. Yoga used to be practiced under strict observation, and was passed on secretly and precisely for a very long time. From generation to generation, it was transmitted from masters to qualified disciples only—those capable of receiving it—[thus assuring its purity remained intact.] Because of that, Yoga was barely known outside of India until Vivekananda introduced it to America at the end of the 19th century. However, once it became known, people were enthusiastic to learn it. Around the time of the large-scale war of the mid-20th century, a great exchange and interaction between all parts of the world rapidly developed, and Yoga was eagerly received and came to be widely practiced. However, after the war, the rapid growth in the popularity of Yoga leaned more toward its material or earthly benefits such as health and beauty—especially when *asana* became its central focus. It is a fact that the sacred scriptures list "slimming of the body," "beautification of the skin," "improved voice" and various other effects as the benefits of *asana* practice. However, they are just temporary side effects and not the ultimate goal. Unfortunately, people seem to be blinded by these effects and have become attached to them.

All in all, *asana* must be correctly understood in its original form, as it has been carefully taught since ancient times. Our Yoga practice also contains *asana*, but it should be finished quickly and swiftly. If the body becomes a strong, healthy yogic body, *asana* has served its purpose. Any attachments to the beautification and health of the body beyond what is necessary has an adverse effect. Meditation is then practiced so that the original goal of Yoga is fulfilled. I am not sure if we can say it is a unique characteristic, but if we are drawing comparisons with the mission of Shri Ramakrishna, you may find a slight difference. I do consider the system of Yoga that includes *asana* to be the primary and complete system of Yoga, for it contains *all* the paths of Yoga—*raja yoga**, *jnana yoga**, *bhakti yoga** and *karma yoga**. This aspect of our practice, which originally was nothing extraordinary and actually quite traditional, might look unique in the current time.

To sum it up, Yoga is universal. "Universal" means that the contents of Yoga are for all, with no discrimination in its teachings and methods. It need not be said that the Truth is always the same; it is changeless. It is One. Yoga is for the realization of this.

IV

Mind and Supreme Bliss

(Friday, 10 May 2002, New York City)

It's around 7:50 pm when the disciples who are visiting from Japan arrive at Sufi Books, where satsangha *is to take place. The space is already filled with sacred peacefulness, inducing a revered silence in everyone. The atmosphere is quite different from the dignified mood of the asana and meditation classes. This mood seems to flow directly from the aspirations of all the seekers who have gathered for* satsangha *tonight. The sheepskin for Shri Mahayogi is placed at the head of the room, while a disciple arranges flowers and places them next to the Master's seat. Some attendees are seated and meditating. The disciples work on final preparations for Shri Mahayogi's arrival. Although everyone maintains silence, they are eagerly anticipating* satsangha.

Anandamali announces Shri Mahayogi's arrival, and everyone stands, with palms together, as a sign of respect for the Master. Shri Mahayogi enters, places his palms together with a smile, walks through the space and sits down. It seems everyone is drawn into Shri Mahayogi's eyes.

The Teachings and Their Acquirement
Through Direct Experience

Satsangha *begins with Yashoda reading the transcript of an exchange between a disciple and Shri Mahayogi.*

Yashoda (reading aloud):

"*Disciple:* As a new student of Yoga, I was introduced to many teachings and did not understand the importance of all of them, and I am still trying to understand the *need* to understand.

"Some people do not accept everything they are taught without understanding the *need* to understand. In other words, it is difficult for me to have "faith"—to believe those things which I cannot experience. To me, one cannot have true knowledge without having both the theoretical knowledge and the experience that verifies the teaching."

Yashoda (now reading the Master's response):

"*Master:* Very well, that is fine. However, you must experience. And as your experience deepens, true faith emerges.

"Yoga does not demand blind faith; rather, Yoga teaches that one should concretely deepen one's intuition through the experiences emerging from one's own practice. [In Yoga] it is also understood that the result of what one intuits depends on the quality of one's mind. In order to heighten that quality, one must proceed with one's study and one's self-discipline. If the process of deepening continues endlessly, it is inevitable that one must eventually reach perfection, or the Truth. The Truth taught in *The Universal Gospel of Yoga* is not my personal notion or ideology. It was the Truth that Awakened Ones discovered over the span of thousands of years. You don't need to memorize the teachings word for word, but you must bear them in your mind. The Truth is not only for the East, nor is it limited to the Buddha or Shri Ramakrishna. The Truth is universal.

"For instance, there is the [Yoga] precept* of non-killing or non-violence. Why is it that violence or killing is unacceptable? Is it because it is a crime? Because it is a social evil? Or is it because it is unethical or immoral? It is for none of these reasons. There is a teaching based upon the Truth, which says, "All sentient beings are equal, and equally precious. Therefore, no one has any right to hurt anyone or anything." However, in actual society, violence prevails. It results in the suffering and misery we see all around us. All this [suffering and misery] is caused by the mind, which has forgotten the Truth and is grounded in ignorance. So do not think that the teachings of Yoga are something special or different. They are the universal Truth, and of course, *your* Truth also. Please reflect and meditate upon this in order to realize it.

"In order to meditate, one must reflect deeply [on Truth] beforehand. In order to reflect deeply, one must first study. In order to study, one must have the enthusiasm to know [the Truth]. Are you really serious and fully dedicated?

"It is possible to explain all aspects of Yoga, including *asanas*, physiologically, psychologically and philosophically —as a science. It is easy to explain them. However, it is more important to experience the positive changes in the body and the mind, rather than to understand them intellectually. Awakening is not simply to know and understand, but to become and to *be* (to acquire through experience). That has been the objective of Eastern spiritual practices for thousands of years. The Truth is within you already, but the movement of the mind keeps you from realizing it. The mind is like wind, the breath is like water, and the body is like ice. They are all H_2O, but it is very difficult to grasp the wind. So, given that ice is the easiest thing to grasp, we control our physical body by practicing *asanas*. Then the breath, likened to water, will obey the body, the vessel. When the breath is controlled, the mind is controlled. Once the mind is still, the True Self is realized —That is *Satori*: Awakening."

Purification of the Mind

Man A: Mahayogi, I want to know the relationship between the purity of the heart and the purity of the body. How does that work? As the body becomes pure does the heart then become pure? Also, what is the heart, and is there perhaps a relationship between the heart, the body and the mind in terms of purity?

Master: The purification of the body in our practice means to have as healthy, strong and flexible a body as possible. Someone may have an illness in the body. However, it does not mean that the body is impure. The body is an instrument. What determines whether the body is pure or not is the mind. So then, purification of the mind is what we must do. What is impurity of the mind? To not know the Truth. This is called ignorance. Therefore, get rid of ignorance swiftly. By doing so, the mind will regain its original purity.

You mentioned the word "heart," but what is your general understanding of the difference between the heart and the mind?

Man A: "The pure heart can see God," and the heart is related to *samadhi**. So I wanted to know—because it is a spiritually important thing—what exactly is the heart from the spiritual perspective?

Master: That is a correct understanding. "Heart" also indicates the physiological heart, and it is understood as the core of a person. Certainly, the heart is a very important part of the mind, which is connected to the center. So then, intensify your heart's passion for the Truth and progress toward Awakening.

Man A: What does the heart have to do with our relationship to *karma**? Is the purity of the heart related to how much *karma* you have left?

Master: Going through the process of purification means to lessen *karma*.

Woman A: Does that mean that *sanskaras** and memory come from the heart?

Master: The vast accumulation of memories from innumerable past lives is called *sanskara*. You should understand that *sanskara* consists of a part of the mind associated with memory, and it affects both the heart and the mind. [The seeds of] good *karma* and bad *karma* all remain latent as *sanskaras*, or memories.

Woman A: Does that mean the purification of the heart is actually ridding oneself of *karma*?

Master: Purification is the imprinting of good *sanskaras* and the eliminating of bad ones. I used the words "good" and "bad." Yoga distinguishes between good and bad as such: Whatever comes from *kleshas** is considered bad, and what does not come from *kleshas*, or helps to remove *kleshas*, is good.

Woman A: Does that happen in the heart? This is a continuation of the question about the heart and *karma*. Is the work [of purification] dealing with memory, because we bring habits with us? Does that mean it is best to meditate on the heart *chakra**? What is the best way to purify?

Master: That is one of the ways. If we speak of "good" or "bad" in a more concrete way, *karma* that follows ego and ignorance becomes bad *sanskara*, and *karma* that follows the Truth becomes good *sanskara*. The latter can also become the power of purification.

The Five Sheaths of Human Beings and Supreme Bliss

Woman B: I heard that there are five sheaths* that constitute the human body. If the innermost sheath is the sheath of bliss, why does it become a hindrance to realizing the True Self?

Master: There is a theory that human existence consists of five sheaths. Some of you may not know about the theory, so I will explain it again.

The outermost sheath is the physical body, which is sustained by food. The sheath that supports the physical body is the vital body, called the *prana** body. The sheath that supports the *prana* body is the mental sheath. The sheath that supports the mental one is the intellect. And the fifth sheath that supports the intellect is the principle of bliss. It is said that the theory of the five sheaths is one of the sacred teachings in the Upanishads*, which has been conveyed for more than three thousand years. To indicate the fifth sheath, bliss, the word *ananda* * is used. The *ananda* in this context has a slightly different meaning from the *Ananda* of *Sat-Chit-Ananda* in *Vedanta*. If *ananda* is translated into modern language, the words "bliss," "happiness" or "joy" are used. If *ananda* refers to *Sat-Chit-Ananda*, *ananda* then becomes *Ananda* with a capital "A." Understand that there is a difference. In this sense, you can understand that the fifth sheath of joy, *ananda*, is a smaller *ananda*, which has derived from *Sat-Chit-Ananda*. So, the capital *Ananda* exists beyond the five sheaths.

(*The woman who asked the question nods in understanding.*)

Man A: I have one more question. I have waited for nine months (*laughing*), so I have a lot of questions! I read that Vivekananda, after Shri Ramakrishna died, was getting more advanced, and he said to the other disciples, "No matter what you can imagine, you can never imagine how great Ramakrishna's consciousness was." I can think that Ramakrishna was capable of being conscious of infinite universes, infinite realms of existence. How much was he aware of? He was supposed to be *Sat-Chit-Ananda* or something.

Master (laughing): I am glad to know that you are studying well. *(laughter from all)*

(Shri Mahayogi interjects, speaking cheerfully but pointedly.)

Is God finite or infinite?

Man A: It is infinite.

Master: Therefore, Ramakrishna is infinite as well.

Man A: OK. My last question: When a person dies do they experience *samadhi*? Or is it something else? I have heard that when you die you experience a tremendous bliss. Is that *samadhi* or something else?

Master: It is true that commonly the word *samadhi* is used when someone passes away. In truth, it is not a proper way to use the term. But, when one finishes one's life, then the next lifetime is promised. How long will the repetition of death and birth continue? It continues until one becomes awakened in *samadhi*.

The Illusion of the Mind and Returning to the Origin

Karuna: Can Mahayogi speak about forgiveness?

Master (after a brief pause): Forgiveness does not need a complex reason or explanation. Truth is One. How can one who forgives and one who is forgiven exist? Forgive the mind, which does not know or understand this.

Man B: How do you forgive the mind, yet protect yourself from being tampered with or damaged by others who maybe don't realize this, and maybe continue to do harmful things?

Master: As I just said, Truth is One. Each person must simply strive to realize it by himself or herself. All and everything is included in that.

Padmini: Can we realize within any circumstance that Truth is One?

Master: It is possible, because the Truth is here and now.

Man C: Why must we experience attachment? I'm wondering why do we become attached to things, objects, people? What is the value, what can we learn from that?

Master: All humanity has been suffering with this issue throughout time. The answer that *yogis* have found is this: the mind mistakenly sees Reality in ephemeral things. Even though the world and the mind itself are impermanent, the mind tries to create reality within them. The Truth, as Reality, is in the innermost Self. The cause of attachment is forgetting the Truth, and seeing non-Truth as Truth. Therefore, when the mind realizes its error, it is the turning point of return to the Truth. The mind feels pained and bound and struggles to become free, even though Freedom or Truth is its original essence. It is as if the mind is playing a monodrama: it binds itself and suffers, then unbinds itself by itself and becomes free.

(The questioner and his friend nod with conviction.)

Man D: Ramakrishna said some negative things about *hatha yoga**. Bodhidharma* encouraged monks to be physically active, and Shri Mahayogi encourages *hatha yoga* up to some point, so there seems to be some contradiction.

Master: Through the ages, awakened beings have descended with respective great missions. It is said that Ramakrishna himself mastered all aspects of *hatha yoga*, but he forbade the practice of it, calling it meaningless. He did not entirely encourage the practice of *raja yoga*, to which *hatha yoga* belongs. As you know, he fervently taught *bhakti yoga*, because it was [and is] the safest and quickest path. Shri Ramakrishna lived in India during the 19th century. India is a very religious country and understands Yoga correctly. However, in the 20th century when Yoga spread across the world, few people understood Yoga properly. Many confused the goal with the means; *hatha yoga* is in fact only a part of the means. The reality of the present situation is that *hatha yoga* is the current fashion in the world, and also *bhakti yoga* is not understood or taught correctly.

Looking at the situation objectively, we realize that it is crucial to set the whole of Yoga straight. Awakening is of the utmost importance. The means may be countless but they are only means, not the goal. Placing the whole of Yoga, including *hatha yoga*, in its proper perspective is what I have been doing. As the sacred scriptures of *hatha yoga* state: "The step [of *hatha yoga*] has to be completed swiftly. Then move forward to *raja yoga*." My role is to mention this and to remind you of it sometimes. (*laughter from Shri Mahayogi and the audience*) There was a long interval between this visit and the last.

Woman C: Is *bhakti yoga* also a method?

Master: It is both the means and the goal.

Woman C: I have one more question that has to do

with the sheaths we talked about before. When you say "mental sheath," do you mean the dualistic mind, our conceptual mind? How do you define that?

Master: All five *koshas** are within duality.

Woman C: All five *koshas* are within the dualistic mind?

Master: Indeed.

Woman C: If there is an underlying sense of oneness, there's no sheath? (*to the translator*) I assume he's saying *koshas* exist within the One Consciousness?

Master: From another perspective, the five *koshas* do not exist. Only One being exists.

Priya: Will Mahayogi please talk to us about the *guru** and disciple relationship?

Master: The original One separated into many. Those who have forgotten the original One try to regain the One. The definitive way to return is given by Truth or the One. Upon return, one realizes there is only One; no longer the many. The relationship between *guru* and disciple exists only in this process. And it is understood that this special relationship endures through countless lifetimes. Needless to say, it is a relationship unlike that of teacher and student in the everyday sense, nor is it one of give-and-take. It only persists by true Love. There is no other word for it.

Man E: Coming back to the original purpose...what is the source of the enthusiasm it takes to generate motivation and energy to work toward Enlightenment? If you don't have enthusiasm, is it because of ignorance or something else?

Master: Yes, ignorance. The practice is the battle against ignorance and *kleshas.*

You may have heard of the caste system in India. There are four main castes. The slavery caste, which merely enjoys sensory pleasures, is the bottom caste. Above that is the commoner caste, which has many ambitions. Above that is the warrior caste, which values justice. And then the highest caste is the *brahmin* or monk caste, which aims for the realization of the Truth. At a glance, it appears as if the caste system only expresses a social structure, but actually it suggests a psychological structure.

The sensual mind, which indulges in emotions, is called a slave. The calculating mind with various self-interests is called a commoner, the realm of most people due to desires or *kleshas.* Those who possess the kind of mind that fights for good religiously and socially and loves the righteous—namely justice—can be called warriors. Internally, the warrior represents the state of battle against the *kleshas* to seek for the Truth. The fourth caste is the mind of the monk who loves and serves the Truth. That is why you must fight. If you don't, you cannot move forward to the fourth.

Man E: Is it okay to enjoy a break? (*Everybody laughs.*)

Master (laughing): Well, even a warrior needs to rest from time to time. (*more laughter from all*) But do not rest for long or you will lose track of your enemy.

Man D: Will Mahayogi talk on a topic of his choosing?

Master (after pausing for a moment): I am always empty. I have no idea what I am going to say. I make no preparations at all beforehand, and I don't even know how I will begin. Today you asked me [some questions] and I spoke a little bit. However, I always think that behind everyone's questions are all my answers. And for all of you who do not know, this voice is being used. The word cannot express what is beyond the word. However, we must use these poor words to indicate That. The role of words is to take the mind to a certain level. When you have reached beyond all limits, the Truth is awakened in you. We meditate in silence so that more of these opportunities can arise.

Let us all enjoy the silence, even in the time when we are not meditating.

(*Long minutes pass in silence. Some attendees receive* darshan *from Shri Mahayogi, at which point tears begin streaming down the face of an attendee.*)

Master (joyously, but in a small voice): Satsangha is wonderful because we can become one with capital "A" *Ananda.*

But the time of *maya** is approaching. Please take the bliss home in your heart. I am looking forward to seeing you again next week.

Satsangha (New York)

V

God and Master

(Friday, 17 May 2002, New York City)

Shortly after Shri Mahayogi's arrival, satsangha *begins with a stream of active questions. Yashoda, the interpreter for this* satsangha, *has brought her parents, who are visiting from Hokkaido, Japan.*

Man A: What is a *paramahansa*? What are the qualifications of a *paramahansa*?

Master: Literally translated, *paramahansa* means "supreme swan." Since time immemorial in India, it has been said that if you give milk mixed with water to a swan, it will only drink the milk. The swan represents the "*hansa**" of *paramahansa*; it takes only the Truth in the world, where good and evil reside together. This title is not given to a holy person by his or her own accord, but is given by another. In order to become a holy person who has the power to embody a *paramahansa*, discipline yourself intensely and attain *Satori*. People will eventually call you a *paramahansa*.

Man B: We all experience the various kinds of chatter from conflicting thoughts in our mind. How does one learn to separate intuition from intellect? How do you learn when to trust yourself, when most of the time this voice is chattering in your head? Which voice should I listen to?

Master: Who is listening to the chatter?

Man B: I am.

Master: Who is the "I"?

Man B: ...I do not know the answer.

Master: Isn't that your Self?

Man B: I guess so, yes.

Master: The chatter of the mind occurs inside and outside the body. Don't pay too much attention to the chatter. Instead, seek your Self, which you have lost.

Man B: How?

Master: Inquire.

Kamalakshi: To continue with this gentleman's question, *The Universal Gospel of Yoga* mentions that we are to align thought, word and deed. When we walk through life, we may think negatively about people or ourselves. What is the way that we can just stop this? What I have been trying to do is to say *Om** to stop it. What are some ways to just stop the thinking from going the wrong way so we can practice day in and day out?

Master: There are two methods: one is to stop the breath. However, there is the possibility that you could die. (*laughter from attendees*) The other method is to stop the mind. If I say that, then you immediately say, "How do I stop the mind?" (*more laughter*) Indeed, due to *sanskaras*, past memories, the mind refuses to stop its activity. The only way to erase *sanskaras* is through the study and practice of meditation in Yoga. I believe that it is the fastest and surest way.

Kamalakshi: The mind, words and actions, they all should become one. So I guess the important thing is to not criticize others, nor criticize yourself, and to just keep the mind pure. That's what I am trying to do, so controlling the tongue, which comes from controlling the mind, is very important.

Master: Yes.

Prajna: Does that mean that we simply have to be patient with ourselves, and continue to practice until the mind becomes more still, that there isn't anything else we can do?

Master: Yes. The rise of the feeling that you have to be patient reveals the fact that there is something in your mind that does not yet allow you to be patient. So to remove the obstacles in the mind, you should be patient with whatever requires your patience. *Satori* will then eventually be attained. This discipline will often create heat in your mind.

Prajna: What will actually create the heat?

Master: Instead of the fire of anger and accusation going outward, the fire is internally contained [and controlled]. From old times, this has been called *tapas**. It is the transformation of impurities into their pure form by thorough burning, just as fire is used for smelting gold from ore.

Meditation on God

Woman A: We all live in the world with different responsibilities. What is the best exercise to do continuously during the day—at work, going home, coming here? What would the Master suggest as the best, the best of the best, besides Yoga [*asanas*], besides waking up in the morning and spending just an hour or half an hour doing it? What would be the exercise that we should do continuously throughout the day?

Master: Meditation on God.

Woman A: How about just practically? (*laughter*)

Master: Go to a business school somewhere. (*Attendees laugh again.*)

Woman A: What about just one exercise? Yoga is an exercise, right?

Master: Yoga is not simply an exercise.

Woman A: I understand, but meditation is exercise, especially in the beginning, isn't it? There are different teachings where the *gurus* suggest different things, some of them more philosophical than practical. Yoga is practical and so is meditation—less of a philosophy and more of a practice. I was just asking for a more practical suggestion.

Master: It is said that Yoga has been in existence for more than 3,000 years. Throughout this long history, the word "Yoga" has been used to indicate *Satori*, or Awakening. What are we awakened to? What must be realized? It is the Truth, the True Self and the Truth of God. Various teachings and methods for *Satori* have been passed on. But is it really possible to realize God through technique alone? If that were the case, then God would be inferior to technique. Can God be realized with intellect alone? If God could be realized by intellect, then God would be inferior to intellect. Knowledge and technique are only for educating the mind, which has lost God, and which has forgotten the True Self. However, the True Self is none other than your Self—within yourself. Then where is God? It is within you. Where is the Truth? It is within you. This is as clear as day. To meditate on God, then, is the most practical thing you can do. Through meditation on God, the mind becomes still, and God emerges of itself. Continue to meditate on God, wherever and whenever.

Man C: Could you please explain how to meditate on God? Do you imagine something in your mind? Do you feel it in your heart? I want to try but I do not know how.

Master: As I just now said, God is Truth itself. God is expressed as the perfection within our innermost Self. Nobody has ever seen God—nobody knows what God looks like, what God's voice sounds like—so I can very well understand your hesitation about how to think about God. Yet, there must be a yearning for something perfect and complete somewhere within your heart. It is, however, still too abstract; it is difficult to keep one's mind upon God because, unless we see the form, we cannot believe.

Here is where that which represents God can take shape in our minds. So have the figures of God-like beings taken shape throughout many religions. If you have faith in a particular religion, then have faith in the image of God within that particular religion. Going further, it is also good to have an image of a *universal* God-like being—that is, an awakened one. Whatever the case may be, find the most certain, ideal image of God. Then, love that form and meditate upon that form.

Woman B: Can prayer be a part of meditation? Can prayer be considered as meditating on God?

Master: Prayer is a part of meditation.

Man B: Is it possible to speak to God directly instead of through prayers? And is there a right or wrong way?

Master: From what I hear, God does not like to bargain.

Man B: What if you are seeking solace, clarity or comfort?

Master: As I just said, to what category does the action belong?

Man B: Sometimes it is a cry for help, I guess.

Master: In that case, God will send you his servant rather than help you directly.

Man B: When you say "servant," what do you mean?

Master: God never bargains. To God, you must simply love and attempt to get closer. Surrender everything to God—your pain, suffering, joy, pleasure, (*solemnly*) and even your life! (*gently*) Can you do that? When you look to God, you must have that kind of sincerity.

Man B: I guess only you know if it is Truth, only you know when you are being sincere.

Master: You are not the judge of that. God is. (*Attendees laugh.*)

Man B: Well, that is good to know. (*more laughter*)

Prajna: Reading Vivekananda's book about *bhakti**, there are different ideas of God—*Atman** and *Brahman** and *Ishvara**. One gets the idea that God is a separate being that can be idealized and for whom we must have devotion, but at the same time, the book also talks about God as within and that we must realize That. You say that no one has ever seen God or spoken to God or heard his voice. But on the other hand, we are also supposed to understand that, in another sense, everything we see is nothing other than God. So how are all of these ideas supposed to be integrated?

Master: Only One thing exists; it is named *God*. That One thing manifests as the many. Though the manifested names and forms vary, what *is* is only that One. That is the Truth. The mind that does not yet understand this sees various forms as separate and numerous entities—"The One is many, and the many are One." In an everyday mathematics class, you would get an "x" mark—a wrong answer—for this. It is often said that the human world and God world are completely opposites, but from the view point of God, "The many are One" is correct because only one exists—ever. It is like the relationship between the ocean and its waves. In seeing the waves, the mind thinks that there are many, but there is only one ocean. To realize this correctly, the principles of *Atman, Brahman* and *Ishvara* are used as representative names of the One, *God*. Therefore, there is no contradiction between the concepts you've mentioned.

Man A: Ramakrishna was aware of everything in the entire universe. I am curious about how the physiological mind and body are able to do something a super-computer cannot do.

49

Master: No matter what discoveries or inventions are made, or how fine a device is created, the eternity that is Shri Ramakrishna allows for the possibility of anything at any time.

Man A: Because he is eternal he can do that? There is something beyond the physical that allows him to do that?

Master: Yes.

Man A: It is said that we only use about 13-14% of the brain. In realization, do we use 100% of the brain?

Master: The correlation between the human brain and realization has not yet been clearly understood [by modern science]. However, there has been a number of awakened ones on this earth. And Awakening is possible for all of us. In fact, we are already awake, even if we only use 13% of our brains. (*laughter from attendees*)

The Necessity of a Teacher (Guru)

Man D: My question is about the role of personal relationships in our spiritual growth. I am a teacher and I have noticed that some of the things I encourage my students to work on are sometimes things I need to hear for myself, as if I am speaking to myself. I am trying to make sense of this and how our relationships can help us to grow.

Master: It is often said that, to teach is to learn. Teachers and students do have differences in their positions, but in terms of human existence they are completely equal. So, although in terms of spirituality the differences between teacher and student are obvious, understand that in all teacher-student relationships—other than a spiritual one—both student and teacher are actually students learning the Truth together. Heighten the sense of humanity in each other; that is, walk together toward the Truth. That is what must be done in all human relationships in the world. We are all learning together.

Man E: My question is simple: How does one find the most important thing one can do in this lifetime?

Master: Ask, then you will be given. Seek, then you will find. Knock, then the door will open.

To realize the True Self, to realize the Truth, to realize God—that is all.

Man E: What is the purpose of realizing the True Self or the Truth?

Master: There is no purpose. (*All laugh.*) It is not about a purpose. It is simply about reclaiming your True Self.

Man F: Is it true that until you realize the True Self you are bound to suffer in different ways?

Master: As long as you think so.

Man C: On the path to realization, is the help of a master necessary, or can one do it alone? Is the help of a master the only way to find the True Self?

Master: A true master is a must.

Man C: Why? Because it is hard or dangerous, or what is it?

Master: If you wanted to acquire knowledge, a technique or whatever it may be, you would go to someone who has mastered it. If you want to attain realization, the safest way is to go to someone who has attained realization. It's as simple as that.

Woman B: It's not that simple—"Go to a master." You may go to a master, but you may feel you are not received or you are not accepted. If you don't have a master, does it mean that you are not ready? What do you do about it?

Master: It may be that either you are not ready or that the relationship is not right.

Woman B: How do you make sure that the relationship is right?

Master: The master must be waiting for the disciple.

Woman A: If the relationship is right, would there be chemistry like falling in love, or would there not be chemistry, because the master is like emptiness, a vast existence? Is there any way to know if the relationship is right?

Master (after a moment of silence): All is by the grace of the master. Meeting your master is exactly like falling in love.

Man B: I am not sure what you are saying. Are you saying that you cannot achieve realization unless you have a *guru* or a master? That seems to limit a lot of people. Not everyone has access to that.

Master: How many people are really, earnestly yearning for Awakening and are looking for a master?

Man B: So ultimately you need a master to get to the final step?

Master: Indeed.

Woman C: What happens after you reach Awakening?

Master: Nothing really. (*Attendees laugh.*) See for yourself sometime.

Man B: Does the past exist, and does it have any bearing on the present?

Master (laughing): Were you born just now?

Man B: No. (*Everybody laughs.*) So, are you saying it *does* exist? (*more laughter*)

Master: Yes, indeed, in your mind.

Man A: I read that the past, the future and the present already exist, but we are just experiencing it within the framework of time and space. All possible futures exist at the same time.

Master: There are many perspectives. From a physical perspective, the hands of the clock separate time into past and future by their movement. From a metaphysical perspective, a big future tree already dwells within its seed. From a psychological perspective, past and future exist in the present at the same time, within the mind.

Kamalakshi: So the practice is to live in the present moment. In order to practice that and to be able to do that continuously, do we have to just do the Yoga that we have to do, or do we keep bringing our mind back to the present moment? Is that what we should do all the time?

Master: What we can do is what we do now.

Kamalakshi: But Yoga will help us to do that more?

Master: Yes. (*pointedly*) Everything exists in the now.

Prajna: Even if we are working towards Awakening

in this lifetime, we may not succeed, in spite of a true desire to do so. But the desire for Awakening can create some *sanskaras* that continue into the next life, from what I understand. If the True Self, the Eternal Self, is already beyond all of that, and the body is transient and the mind changeable, what part is it that continues on to the next lifetime?

Master: That is called the *sukshma**. It is not the gross body, but the subtle mind.

Prajna: But the mind and the ego are not the same.

Master: One of the pillars that constitutes the mind is the ego. The others are intellect, thoughts and memories and so on. All of these combined are what we call the mind.

Prajna: How does this aspect relate to the *prana* body?

Master: The *prana* body is employed when one exits the body [at the time of death]. Also, when the mental body returns in the next life, it creates [the physical] form together with the *prana* body.

Man G: Why do you teach?

Master: I am just enjoying the conversation. (*Many attendees laugh.*)

Man G: Me too. (*more laughter*)

Master: Well, let us enjoy again next time.

VI

Ignorance of the Mind

(Friday, 6 August 2004, New York City)

To introduce this satsangha, *Kamalakshi gives a strong reading of Sananda's article, published in* Paramahaṃsa*, titled "The Yogi's Aim—The Meaning of Life." The article reveals the passion of Sananda, a yogi who practices with serious commitment under the guidance of the Master. He writes: "We should not give up the sincere search for the meaning of life...the methods and discipline of Yoga are open to everyone."*

When Kamalakshi finishes the reading, the space is permeated by silence.

The Deluding Power of Ignorance

Megan: Everything makes sense to me in the article, but it seems that there are some special challenges for householders. This is in terms of the amount of practice that is possible—or a deeper, more total level of commitment.

Master: As Sananda said in his article, he is a householder with a wife and children, who works at a company in Japan. Even in such circumstances, the accomplishment of Yoga is possible.

There are two aspects that must be realized through Yoga. One is the elimination of the ego and *kleshas*, caused by ignorance; that is, non-Truth. The other is the

Awakening into the True Self, actualized when the ego and *kleshas* are eliminated. Only these must be studied and accomplished through Yoga. Other things, like books or practices you find in bookstores or yoga centers, can only minimally help you.

Foremost is the impulse that arises from your heart. The more intense the fire from within your heart, the more quickly you can burn out your ego and *kleshas*. Therefore, Enlightenment is possible for householders, women, men and even children.

Megan: As householders, is there any path of Yoga that leads the family or entire community to Enlightenment, instead of just the committed individual?

Master: When you say "community," a community still consists of individuals, doesn't it? The issue then is whether each individual practices seriously or not. Concretely, you must change yourself first. To do that you need to study the Truth, and discipline yourself according to the teachings. By doing so, as I just said, ego, *kleshas* and desires will be eliminated; then self-sacrifice, or selfless service, appears spontaneously. What a wonderful world it would be if each individual could practice self-sacrifice within a community!

Rafael: I read Ramana Maharshi's book about *jnana yoga*, the path of negation. As a method for accomplishing Enlightenment, do you recommend the inquiry of "Who am I?" as an efficient way to practice?

Master: It is one of the most indispensable paths.

Rafael: In actuality, can one practitioner alone become

adept in this path, or does it require a *guru*, or community?

Master: All that is necessary are the teachings of the Truth and the *guru* who bestows them.

Rafael: How does one receive them?

Master: Ask. Then you shall be given.

Gerald: Mahayogi said, if I have this correct, that the core of one's being is eternal or immortal. My question is: How does one experience that? It is not the thought, the emotion or the sensation. Is there another type of experience that we don't know about yet?

Master: Indeed, it is strange. **The realization of the True Self is already within all, right here and now.** You yourself don't know it—that is to say, there seems to be something obstructing and hiding it. That [obstacle] is verily the mind; it is the thought, it is the emotion, it is the experience. Therefore, all you need to do is to eliminate the obstacle.

Thoughts have deep roots within the mind. They are based upon memories from the past, which are called *sanskaras*. The mind can be compared to a camera and a film. The experiences of many lifetimes are automatically burned onto the film. Of course, each individual has different memories—as the tastes and tendencies of each individual differ, so do the objects that are projected [onto the mind]. After many previous lifetimes, one is born again into this lifetime, and once again, through actual experiences, past memories [of the mind] instantly reappear in this world. If you try to trace back further to the cause of these impressions—likes or dislikes, or the objects the mind desires—you will find the workings of the mind attempting to project something within this world as the *original* cause.

However, this world is impermanent; it changes, and limitations come. All sorts of worldly dreams are always broken in the process. Even if you seek happiness or pleasure, the end is always suffering. No matter how immense the happiness you obtain, the god of death always wins. Pain will be created in direct proportion to the happiness you have gained.

This comes from the mistake of trying to see the Truth in this world, which is like a phantom—the mistake of expecting to obtain happiness from it, and the mistake of identifying oneself with the mind and the mind's possessions. This can be clearly understood using scientific reasoning. However, it seems that the power of *sanskaras* created in the past always wins over the intellectual mind. This power, which covers the Truth, is called ignorance. Thus, all you must do is **eliminate ignorance**, which includes the ego.

Do not worry at all. This is not about "losing yourself" (*laughing*). It is about realizing your True Self. There is no other way to awaken to your True Self or the Truth of the entire universe but this.

Gerald: Is the elimination you speak of more like fighting and overcoming it, or can one just walk away from it, leaving it aside?

Master: Truly, how easy it would be for you if you could move forward toward Enlightenment smoothly, but—

Gerald (interjecting):—Is it easy to walk out of it or just leave it to the side and…?

Master: Surely it is easy, if you can do it. But no single person ever has. (*Everybody laughs.*) It always involves an intense battle. However, if you confront it and practice seriously and passionately, you will definitely win your way through. Above all else, always remember that the Truth is in your heart, in the core of you.

That is your True Self.

Gerald: Is it enough to practice by focusing on the heart, as opposed to dealing with all these thoughts and objects? Where do I put my energy, my focus or concentration?

Master: Really focus on the core with all your heart, so much so that you would give up your life for it.

(*Gerald is speechless. Others react with laughter.*)

One more guarantee: When you finally do give up your dear life, immortality will be obtained.

Our essence is **Eternal Existence**. It is unborn, without death. That is truly the only thing that exists.

Often in this world, we use the words "reality," "existence," or "consciousness" but none of these are eternal existence. To be accurate, none of these are Reality or Existence at all. The essence of your self, however, is that very Reality.

Priya: A few years ago, I came to speak with you about adopting a child. Well, it came through. So, my question is, now what should I do? (*All laugh.*)

I've found much meaning in the work I do because

for me it is the environment of *Om Tat Sat**. I realize that a child takes a lot of focus and concentration, so I want to know how *bhakti yoga* and *karma yoga* relates with *pratyahara**. I want to do the best I possibly can with the child and of course maintain my practice for myself and also for her. So in terms of truth, it seems that there are so many things one needs to deal with for a child, things that in some ways I want to drop. But still, it is important to help somebody else who is suffering. What would you tell me is the best way to do all these things?

Master: You are definitely not a superwoman (*laughing*), so you should not think that you have to do everything perfectly. Understand that the situations you are given, whatever they may be, are all opportunities for your *sadhana**, so serve those who are suffering—the child, and of course, your husband. Whatever the task is, and regardless of the action you take, everything is Yoga.

This is the secret of *bhakti yoga* and *karma yoga*.

Kamalakshi: I have heard of the Buddhist practice of mindfulness. Can mindfulness lead to Enlightenment?

Master: By "mindfulness," do you mean always and constantly making the effort to observe your thoughts, words and actions?

Kamalakshi: To always live in the moment, that is the practice. To live in the present, aware of presence. With every step, feeling the presence, you know, that you are walking.

Master: Well, it is a very basic and important teaching. It means firmly controlling all your actions, including your thoughts, and mastering them. By practicing this, desires or *kleshas* that are caused by ignorance are restrained. Beyond that, I have already told you.

Kamalakshi: Really going to the aim.
(Shri Mahayogi gazes upon Kamalakshi and nods.)

Man A: I agree with everything that has been said, and I like to be reminded of all this, of course, but I find myself either too modest, or too limited, or actually not courageous enough to really want to attain the True Self. I know I should. That is not all; *passion*, that is the thing. I really try not to have too much energy that could cause me trouble. What should I do?

Master: I don't know!
(All laugh for some time, then silence ensues.)

Master: How long do you think you are going to live?

Man A: I have no idea.

Master: Right. Death comes suddenly.

Man A: I am so afraid that I don't even want to think about it.
(Shri Mahayogi looks at him and smiles.)

Love and Non-Attachment

Rafael: When you renounce your life, do you renounce your children, your wife, your love for the world? Do you renounce what you do professionally, or as an occupation?

Master: You can't renounce your current obligation, which is to support your family. What must be renounced is the false attachment to family.

Rafael: Is love false?

Master: Love is one of the manifestations of what is right. Therefore you must fulfill your obligations all the more.

Priya: At the last *satsangha*, Shri Mahayogi talked about love. You said something about love being most powerful, and that love does not expect anything in return. Here, we are also talking about love without attachment. I feel, though, that there are differences in love, but I am not clear what they are.

Master: Usually, love has hate as its shadow side. But True Love has no shadow. It is to give oneself up entirely. Even if one's family is founded on loving relationships, it is still a device for learning how to love. Love does not grow into True Love unless you make it grow. To do so, you must learn what True Love is and practice it. What I said to him (*meaning Rafael*) includes this.

Of course, the closer you get to True Love, the more the ego and *kleshas* fade. It indicates that the mind is approaching preparedness to realize the Truth.

Priya: Sometimes, very often when I am dealing with people, I try practicing unconditional Love, love without the shadow side. But sometimes I feel that a more productive interaction with another person can be had if I show my ego. A few emotions or disagreements come up, and although it requires my effort, I know we go through something together, and then sometimes, I come out with a little less shadow than I tried to go in with.

I am not perfect yet, but I try to make my best effort—unconditional, unattached—but my husband says, "Get real!" or somebody else says, "Come on, become involved in a more attached way," yet they are not necessarily practicing Yoga.

Master: If you are really dealing with others through True Love, no matter what kind of reaction you receive you will not be affected by it. So you must not think of it as an issue.

Kristin: Is the diminishment of suffering the main sign that the ego is dying properly?

Master: Yes.

Kristin: And how do you know the difference between the absence of suffering and the presence of mere pleasure? Pleasures or comforts are not the opposite of suffering, are they? It often seems to me that worldly pleasures are just fine, and I like them, so how do I distinguish between true joy and pleasure?

Master: The mind never learns its lesson no matter how many times it experiences pleasure and suffering. The pleasures of the world might be pleasurable within it, but how many hours do they last, how many minutes? The next moment the suffering of loss appears, and then the mind seeks out a new pleasure. Pleasures are not eternal, so the suffering [of loss] and seeking [of pleasure] keeps repeating.

True happiness comes as the absence of suffering in reaction [to dualistic conditions.]

Kristin: That is the end of craving pleasures?

Master: Yes. Seek eternal pleasure rather than limited pleasure.

Kamalakshi: You said that pleasure and pain are equal, didn't you?

Master: Yes.

Kamalakshi: I just wanted to make sure. (*All laugh.*)

Master: Yes, I said "directly proportional."

Kamalakshi: So, if not in this life, then in the next life?

Master: It is so.

Megan: About pains, pleasures, God-Love and the shadow side of love: In my life, the relationships in which I feel the most intense love are with my family. Even though I try to make the context of my life very much a *karma yoga* type of situation, service to the people I love has a shadow side. I see it and I can recognize it, but it's hard to control. At a certain level, loving them gives me something—a mirror to see with. My family is my love, yet I can only see my attachment to them. It's not pure service, just because I still feel that I have not yet completely let go of expecting my child to be certain ways, or my husband to be certain ways.

Master: Right, the family is the most wonderful place for self-discipline. Of course, there are many situations that will arise. However, you must not complain, but simply and silently continue your *sadhana.*

Megan: It gets better as I get older.

Master: Yes. Perhaps your experiences themselves have been a good *guru* as well.

Each of you, too, will one day eventually part from your family. However, each and every one of your family is the same *Atman*, as you yourselves are.

Megan: The process of letting go is difficult, but I know, in a deep sense, that I must do so.

Master: That's right.

Prajna: If there is a tendency to seek Enlightenment in past lifetimes, does the desire to end the ignorance, the desire for the Truth, also continue from past lives?

Master: Yes. (*smiling*) Otherwise, you would not be here now.

Radha: Shri Mahayogi, you have been coming here to us for 8 or 9 years now. The very first year, you talked about the requirements and responsibilities of disciples. Will you refresh us? (*All laugh.*) There are a lot of new faces.

Master: "*Guru*" and "disciple" in Yoga are not meant to be used the same way as "teacher" and "student" are used in ordinary contexts.

The direct meaning of *guru* is "the light that removes darkness;" that is, the Truth that removes ignorance. The light of the Truth exists within all of you. There is only a little shadow that hinders you. Because of this, sometimes you require a light from outside. The period before the darkness is removed is called *discipleship*. Once it is removed, the difference between the *guru* and disciple no longer exists. They are the same One. Therefore, for the time being, I will speak about the *guru* and the disciple from the viewpoint of differing roles (*smiling*).

First, the disciple must seek *Satori*.

Then, the disciple must learn the teachings of the Truth—the right teachings—from a true *guru*.

Furthermore, the disciple must put the teachings and disciplines into practice earnestly and passionately. This should be the fundamental state of the mind and [the purpose behind your] actions.

If I may say it more particularly: be tractable and humble.

(Attendees become very quiet and noticeably indrawn.)

Master (laughs): What's wrong? (*All laugh.*) Whenever I say this, I always recall the words of Jesus Christ. It is written in the Bible that he also always mentioned something very similar.

Additionally, serve the *guru* and all of creation.

If each one of you truly values yourself, if you value your family and other people, then you will definitely reach the Truth—if you practice keeping in mind what I mentioned.

Shri Mahayogi spends a few moments quietly offering darshan to each attendee. He then says in a light tone, "I will see you again in two weeks."

Inspirited by the grace of the guru, all place their palms together and bow with heartfelt gratitude and respect.

VII

Self-Realization and Freedom

(Friday, 20 August 2004, New York City)

Shantipada opens the satsangha *with a reading of Sananda's article, "Karma Yoga—The Secret of Work." His voice projects strong conviction. Sitting in the front row is Swami Ramananda from Integral Yoga Institute. Although he has visited Shri Mahayogi privately at The Cave*, he has not attended a public* satsangha *in quite some time. Feeling overwhelmed by the company of Shri Mahayogi, and the seekers around him, tears roll down his cheeks.*

As the reading ends, the space is filled with a soft, sacred stillness that lasts several minutes.

The Realized State of Freedom and Supreme Bliss

Anjali: Shri Mahayogi, could you speak more about Enlightenment and freedom as the aim of practice? For it seems that without meeting an enlightened being, one does not get a taste of how great the goal is, nor receive inspiration for the practice. Could you speak about what freedom and Enlightenment are, so that it can motivate people?

(After a moment of silence...Shri Mahayogi answers.)

Master: Everyone wants freedom. Everyone wants

happiness. From the day a person is born until the day a person dies, she or he exerts effort to gain both. Can they be gained by wealth? or by fame? or beauty? or knowledge? Even if you had all of these available to you, because of death, disease and aging, all of them will turn into suffering in an instant. Even if you think you have gained freedom and happiness through these things, the mind is never satisfied by them, for the world is not everlasting. Neither is the world pure, nor perfect. And, by identifying yourself with possessions you think you have gained, you get lost from your True Self.

Why, then, are people destined to seek for freedom and happiness again and again, lifetime after lifetime? If you consider this from a broader perspective, there must be something that nature is teaching us. Thousands of years ago, *yogis* in India unraveled the secret. But it is not just in India; the search for freedom and happiness is universal, independent of religion or nationality.

The conclusion is that freedom and happiness are not outside of the mind, but within the mind. Freedom does not mean that you get whatever the mind desires. Freedom is the state of not being bound by anything. "Not bound" means not dependent on anything. It is the state of true independence. And in that state, there is bliss—the ultimate happiness. Bliss is the state of no suffering and no pain. Yes, this must be what everyone yearns for. Through simply correcting wrong viewpoints, you will be able to realize this.

In Yoga, the conclusion is this: human suffering is caused by ignorance. One kind of ignorance is **seeing permanence in impermanence**. Indeed, our bodies, nature, all of the material world, have limits. Perfect satisfaction cannot be found in any of them. But by seeking bliss within, you can eliminate wrong viewpoints and realize the Truth.

[Another kind of] ignorance is **mistaking the Self** for what is not the Self; the mistake of thinking your ego is your Self. The True Self is inward, farther beyond the ego; that is, the ego is witnessed by the True Consciousness. Isn't it so, that you can in fact know your mind? Yes, the knowing Consciousness is further within the mind. It cannot be moved; it is always Absolute Consciousness. However, a mistake unfortunately arises—that of identifying yourself as the mind. You then think that it is *you* who are happy or unhappy, and this way you struggle. Throughout your lifetime it is very difficult to emancipate yourself from this mistake and this struggle. But if you try again and again, throughout lifetimes, you are destined to arrive closer to the Truth. Yoga speeds the journey. Paramahansa Yogananda once said that when you leave the journey of your soul up to the nature of reincarnation, it's like walking, but in Yoga, it's like taking an airplane to the goal. (*Attendees nod and laugh. Shri Mahayogi laughs.*) Back in those days, the propeller airplane may have been the fastest thing available. Nowadays with the advancements of science, it is possible to go even faster. Of course, this swiftness only occurs if you practice Yoga seriously and earnestly.

Also, please remember that the state of Enlightenment, which is [perfect] freedom and bliss, is expressed by the word "*Nirvana**." This is the ultimate state realized by the Lord Buddha.

The literal translation of *Nirvana* is "the state in which the flame has been extinguished." The flame refers to our life and mind—restless in nature's realm. It flickers and is gone. The mind is likened to a flame. The extinction of the unrest caused by desires arising from ignorance is the state of perfect tranquility called *Nirvana*. In modern days, *Nirvana* may be understood in Yoga as *Nirvikalpa Samadhi**. It is the state of Truth beyond duality, our essence, and the Truth of each one of us. It is here that freedom and bliss reside.

We must wake up to **That**—like oneself awakening to one's Self. It cannot be realized through the intellect. The intellect can take you only so far, but *passion* is more indispensable. You definitely need the passion that makes you stake your life on It [*Satori*]. Then, you will realize Immortality. You must "die" in order to reach the Immortal (*smiling*). Therefore, remove the fear of death in meditation. All arises from the mind.

Truth exists as it is, alone. It does not depend upon intellect or words. Realize That.

The Grace of the Guru

Swami Ramananda: My question is about coping with painful emotions; for example, depression, fear or anxiety, and knowing that it is unhealthy to repress them, but not wanting to fuel them either. Could you speak about a healthy approach?

Master: Everyone here has a variety of differences, perhaps in hobbies or other character traits. These traits were not created today or yesterday. They were created over a long span of time. *Karma* refers to action and reaction. These also have causes within the mind. The causes, traced back to your memories, are called *sanskaras*. The traits you have just mentioned are included as *sanskaras*. How then are *sanskaras* improved? If you have negative *sanskaras*, they will be decreased by applying positive *sanskaras*; if there is a "minus," add a "plus." Concretely, all the *sadhanas* of Yoga assist this process. However, *sanskaras* issue forth strongly from the mind. As this happens, what is most effective is to bow in surrender before the altar dedicated to your *guru*. If you do so, through the love and power that is absolute, your *guru* will uplift you. It is imperative not to give *sanskaras* a chance to come forth.

Alberto: What should I do in order not to give them a chance?

Master: When emotions rise to the surface of the mind, immediately sit before your altar. The altar is not only in your living room or bedroom. If you have true respect and faith in your *guru*, the *guru* is always in your mind. No matter where you go, the *guru* is always within you. But prior to this state, you can gaze at a drawing or photo of your *guru* in front of you wherever you are. You can practice this way anywhere.

Alberto (pointing to Shri Mahayogi's picture in his wallet): How about in the wallet? (*Attendees laugh.*)

Master: That's fine too (*laughing*). Do this to restrain negative emotions from running rampant.

Prem: This question is about meditating on the *guru*. You mentioned that the deeper the meditation, the calmer the mind. But it seems that as the practice deepens, attachment to the object of meditation can prevent the mind from quieting down. It seems that attachments

71

prevent this by perpetuating the constant thought of "I am concentrating," and it seems that this is very difficult to transcend.

Master: This is not a problem; the truth of the *guru* is not the shape of its form, but its **essence**. It is Existence itself—the Truth, which is beyond form and word. It is the same as the Truth within you. The concerns you have will therefore naturally disappear.

Karuna: Again, regarding meditation, this has to do with meditation as an approach to dealing with an active mind. In meditation, there is a search, not necessarily for the Truth, but for safety. I learned a way of meditation from Vietnamese Buddhism in which you say to yourself, "I am home, I am home," and then you seek to "come home." Through this you create feelings of safety or being in "a safe place." I would like to know if this equates to the meditation that Mahayogi recommends, or if it points in a different direction.

Master: The Buddhist method you mentioned is a kind of *mantra yoga**. *Mantra** is not only [practiced with] the word "*Om.*" Any word can be a *mantra*, no matter what the word. There is often a tendency in Buddhism to be somewhat thought or idea oriented, so I do not really advise escaping into a created state of mind. It is rather more correct to say that the mind never has a "home." It is important to entirely abandon whatever materiality the mind wants.

Karuna: Both externally and internally?

Master: Yes, both. The only thing that the mind should depend on is the *guru* and his or her words of Truth.

Radha: Could you please speak about the objects of meditation?

Master: The objects of meditation should simply be the **Truth, God,** or the **True Self**. That's it.

Woman A (first time attendee): I have been on the spiritual path for 15 years and it seems like "[I take] one step forward, two steps back." I need devotion and discipline. I have been very distracted by family, work and environment. I need your guidance and help to lift me out of this cycle so that I can live by the teachings I receive.

Master: As written in Sananda's article that was read earlier, we are all in a similar situation. However, spiritual progress is possible, and Enlightenment is possible.

What is important is to discern between what is the Truth and what is not the Truth, and to understand it correctly and thoroughly. You can learn from *satsanghas* like this, or through reading scriptures. Next, comprehend their teachings correctly, and meditate. Meditation contains the power of discrimination between what is Truth and what is not Truth, and eliminates the false attachments in the mind. If you practice, you will surely feel progress in your spiritual development. As you yourself said, deepen your devotion to the Truth and to your *guru*.

Egil: How do you know the difference between what is your personal *dharma**, to be fulfilled in this life, and what is caused by mere attachment?

Master: There are two understandings of the word *dharma*. One is "duty," which is perhaps what you are referring to by *dharma*. The other is "Truth."

73

In Buddhism, the word *Dharma** [with a capital D] denotes the Truth. It means the absolute Truth. If absolute order can be attained in the universe, then one's *relative* duties in the world must also be founded upon absolute *Dharma*. Until dharma is established in Truth, *dharma*, as relative duties, is governed by *karma*. Yoga transcends *karma*. Since *dharma* in the relative sense that I just mentioned, always changes, then rather than worry about it, focus on *Dharma*, meaning the Truth. Once you are established in the *Dharma* of Truth, then bring relative *dharma* in compliance with it.

The meaning of *dharma* is far-reaching and difficult to understand. However, the original meaning of *dharma* refers to the foundation or support of all things. This relative universe is supported by absolute principles, or laws of Truth.

Woman A: From listening to you tonight, I gather that I have to make offerings to the *guru*, offering everything— suffering, pain, health challenges or emotional issues. Is my understanding correct that I just have to give it all up?

Master: Regardless of what you give up or offer, advance closer to your true nature, which is freedom and bliss.

Waking up to the True Self

Man A: I have a simple question: What is meditation? How should one meditate?

Master: The Truth is already within you. If you have not yet perceived it, you must remove any obstacles to it. Simply speaking, meditation is to destroy the obstacles and, at the same time, to realize the Truth.

Man A: I often hear, "Meditate, meditate," but how should one meditate? Watching myself, or what is it? To imagine something?

Master: Who are you?

Man A: That's the question that one should ask?

Master: Answer it yourself.

Man A: I don't know who I am, that's why I'm here now. (*All laugh.*)

Master (laughing): That is very strange! Indeed, that is really strange. You all must know who you are, though when the question is posed nobody knows the answer! Well, this is the key point. Inquire: "Who am I?"

Alberto: Of the three different kinds of meditation you mentioned, how do you know which one to choose?

Master: Each method is distinct.

By meditating on the **Truth**, you lose ignorance in the mind.

By meditating on **God**, you know the Truth of God.

By meditating on "**Who am I**"? you abolish the false self and wake up to the True Self.

[As you continue to practice] you may proceed to combine them. This does not mean to combine the methods during one meditation; it means to apply one method in one meditation, and then to apply another at another time as necessary.

(Kashinatha arrives with his young daughter and they sit quietly on the floor near the entrance.)

(After a brief pause, Shri Mahayogi begins to speak more slowly.)

Master: The mind is in constant movement, and that movement disturbs it. Still the mind's fluctuations by studying the Truth with passion. If the state of stillness is solidly sustained, you will awaken to the True Self. It is truly a distinct Awakening *(smiling)*. Until then, you are only dreaming.

Woman B: Does the heart play any role in meditation?

Master: Yes, the role of the heart is very big. The passion that I mention again and again arises from the heart. Intensify the heat [of passion] more and nourish it. The waves of the mind will then be calm. The heart is the pathway to the center.

Karuna: In meditation, when I ask, "What is Truth?" or "What is God?," it seems that it is a very verbal thing. Can you let the words go at some point, or if there are no words, is it always best to repeat the words?

Master: Words are grosser aspects of thought. The role of words appears only in the beginning, but once the words penetrate the heart, words are no longer necessary. Then taste and savor it. God is beyond words, but you can still feel it. I want you to feel it and taste it.

Kashinatha (joyfully): It was very important for me to bring my daughter, Adriana, with me today to meet Mahayogi. She asked me on the way over here if you were "Lord." *(Everyone laughs.)* I was at a loss for words because I didn't have the right words. Can you comment?

(Everyone smiles and turns toward little Adriana who clings to Kashinatha.)

Master (smiling): Well, tell her, "Yes!" *(All laugh.)* And say, "Kashinatha, your daddy, is making an effort to become one too. And, Adriana, you yourself are Lord too."

(Kashinatha delightfully conveys Shri Mahayogi's words to Adriana, who is still very bashful.)

Kashinatha: She is very thirsty, so I will have to go get her some water now. I'm sorry! *(laughter from everyone)* It was very important for me to bring her tonight. Thank you!

Woman C: In relation to a question that was previously asked, I tried to practice the "Who am I?" meditation and it wasn't beneficial. Sometimes answers come to me, but it seems as if the repetition of the words prevents the consciousness from expanding.

Master: Very strange. *(Attendees laugh.)*

(Shri Mahayogi, smiling, continues to speak light-heartedly while everyone listens with full attention.)

"I" is Reality itself! It is not abstract—what is abstract is the mind. **You are Reality itself.** Exert a little more effort and continue.

The search should not be taken up with tension in the mind. Do it without heaviness. As Buddha said, "To create a good sound, the string of the instrument is neither too tight nor too loose." The importance is in the tuning. Through continuous training, you will acquire it. Learning, *asanas*, meditation—all is practice, training, and discipline. But you see, these are not the aim—they

77

are the means. Definitively, the aim is to realize the Truth. Therefore, always keep your eyes on the aim.

Anjali: To "stake your life on Realization," does that mean that when one sits down for meditation, one should be willing to die in that moment, physically die?

Master: Although you can *think* it, to truly *do* it is very difficult. Earnestness means to have firm determination—enough to give up one's life if one cannot realize the Truth.

An old story goes that a young practitioner was wandering in the forest, seeking the Truth. A huge monster then appeared, singing the Truth. (*All laugh.*) The seeker instinctively felt, "This monster knows the Truth. I must know this Truth by any means!" The monster said to him, "In exchange for your life, I will teach you." The practitioner told the monster that if he realized the Truth, he would not need life. The monster then taught the young practitioner the Truth. The practitioner immediately realized it, and at that very moment the monster transformed into its original God-nature. It is like that.

May your earnestness and passion for Enlightenment intensify and deepen more and more, to realize the Truth.

Today our time has come to a close—to be continued in two weeks. The continuation of the article "Karma–Yoga," which was read in the beginning, will be read. I am looking forward to seeing you again. Thank you.

Shri Mahayogi ends his talk jovially and exits the space as all attendees stand up, palms together, gazing at the Master with fascination. After his departure, the atmosphere is charged with enthusiasm for Realization, and hearts are filled with reverence for Shri Mahayogi and recommitted with passion for the Truth.

VIII

Compassion and Devotion

(Friday, 3 September 2004, New York City)

A translation of Sananda's article from Paramahaṃsa,
*"Karma Yoga—Self-Sacrifice," is read aloud by Shantipada.
Some of us read along from a leaflet while others listen
with closed eyes as Shri Mahayogi silently gazes upon each
bestowing darshan.*

After the reading, a tranquil silence ensues.

Compassion and Devotion Through Service

Filomena: I wonder if Shri Mahayogi could talk about
the role of compassion and detachment in *karma yoga*.

Master: The article read at the last *satsangha*, "Karma
Yoga—The Secret of Work," was about carrying out your
own duties in service to others. The article read today is
about taking more initiative in devoting yourself to others.

Our ordinary minds are attached to "**me**" and
"**mine**"—the greatest of attachments. In contrast, there
are teachings that require the active practice of *karma
yoga*. When your practice has not yet deepened, you
have to continue carrying out your *karma*, or duties. But
as your practice progresses, you come to realize that the
attachment to "me" and "mine" is a mistake and, at the
same time, sympathy for the pain or sadness of others
wells up in your heart. More advanced *karma yoga* at this
point can begin.

Actively eliminating one's own ignorance and *kleshas* while at the same time selflessly serving others is just as difficult a *sadhana* as that of *yogis* who devote themselves completely to meditation. For example, *raja yogis** realize the Truth through the disciplines of *asana*, *pranayama* and meditation while intensively practicing the precepts [of Yoga.] This is, so to speak, the endeavor to render the mind transparent.

*Karma yogis**, however, achieve the same results through serving others in this world, rather than using the method of meditation. Compassion arises naturally as the result of *karma yoga*.

For your reference, the word *bodhisattva** originated from Buddhist teachings about two thousand years ago. It characterizes the Lord Buddha's discipline in his former lives, and the virtues which resulted from that discipline.

He was born about 2,500 or 2,600 years ago, and then became the Buddha. The *bodhisattva* discipline taught in Buddhism, even two thousand years ago, is to "*devotedly sacrifice yourself for others, and in so doing, sacrifice even your own Enlightenment.*" This teaching is not exclusive to Buddhism. It has been conveyed in India since ancient times, and appears to have existed elsewhere.

So, there is really no separate thing that is "me" or "mine." The only thing there is, is **You**; there is only One Existence.

Woman A: Often when you are at your lowest point and you are faced with fear, it is challenging to have the courage or faith to be able to reach out to someone else, when you feel you have nothing yourself. Maybe you can discuss how you find that strength within yourself.

Master: That is the problem. Certainly, faith is the hope that can lead to infinite possibility; nevertheless, faith needs to be cultivated. To do so, you must study the Truth and train yourself a bit. You can apply any [of the Yoga disciplines]; you can practice *karma yoga* as was mentioned before, or you can practice *asana* or meditation. If you do, then your capacity to understand the Truth will develop, and at the same time your faith will grow stronger. Faith must be based on the Truth; it cannot be a superficial faith based on [a desire to] gain worldly benefits. Therefore, there is a necessity to study the Truth.

The Truth is already within you.

Suzan: Thank you for the last *satsangha*. You said something about remaining calm, and it was very helpful. I am constantly very troubled by the suffering and death our government causes to the people of the world. I wonder if you have any suggestions of how one can help stop this.

Master: Truly, the various events that are happening in the world right now can deepen our sadness. The egos of various countries are the very cause. I wish that the heads of each country, kings or prime ministers, would learn Yoga. (*All attendees laugh.*) But it seems they are only trying to satisfy their desires, rather than trying to make peace.

What can we really do? I think that the basic thing is for each and every person to live righteously, and to continue striving to uplift oneself by having an ideal of a world filled with universal love and peace. Then, find the opportunities to protest, as this is the basis of democracy. What is important is not to become more agitated and confused by what is going on in the world. The thoughts in your mind are more powerful than your words or actions. So always control your mind, filling it with peace and love.

Man A: I understand that *karma yoga* is a wonderful spiritual practice. I try to do my best, but I struggle with people who are unaware of their suffering. I did things for someone, which I thought he would appreciate, but instead it became troublesome, and in the end, I became angry with him. Ultimately, what I want is peace of mind. How does this work?

Master: Karma yoga is to give yourself to others. Do not have angry reactions.

Man A: Can I get hurt mentally from taking abuse from people?

Master: You must create a mind that does not react. Whatever [path of] Yoga one practices, Yoga means to restrain the mind.

The Eternal Being

Gerald: Shri Mahayogi often gives us the words "immortal" or "eternal," as if the only thing that can be true or real is that which is immortal or eternal. What is "eternal" or what is "immortal"? I wonder if you could talk more about that and how it relates...(*pausing*) I think it is more of a psychological phenomenon, that in sudden moments of intensity or concentration, time and the thought of things can stop—right in the midst of the thoughts. Then there is a period where time doesn't exist, and then it exists again.

Master: These words express *Satori*. Time depends on the mind. This is why during pleasurable experiences time seems short, and during difficult ones it seems long. In concentration and meditation, the sensation of time begins to disappear. When you have meditated well, time seems short and when you have not, time seems long. These [perceptions] are still within the realm of the mind.

Satori is beyond the mind. "Beyond the mind" means that the mind's activity comes to a complete stop and the mind itself seems to disappear. At that moment, the Truth is revealed. The Truth is what exists as our essence. Naturally, it cannot be expressed with words. However, the only mode of expression we have is words. The word that best describes it is simply "Existence." "Existence" means **Reality**. It is unrelated to anything else; that is, it is never born and never dies. Thus, it is called "**eternal**" or "**immortal**."

Each and every moment, this body and mind are born and die. But the essence never dies and, of course, the essence is only One—not plural. There is only That. The forms and shapes of the universe may be various, but only on the surface. In the essence, there is only One Reality.

Gerald: So, is the essence the process of trying to identify the concept "I"?

Master: Yes. When we say "I," it refers to the first person. We should then know what this "I" is. Experiences in the world are complex. Relative relationships are not eternal, yet through them we long for absolute love and peace. This is what Truth reveals as the wrong view.

(Gerald, with sincere eyes, continues further.)

Gerald: Does "wrong view" mean to look for perfect love [in this world]?

Master: Yes. Therefore, you must withdraw yourself into the first person—not the second person or third person. Further, continue to go deeper within.

Gerald: What happens to the world when you are going in?

Master: As attachments cease, accordingly, the world gradually disappears. After all, the world is perceived due to our attachments.

Woman A: Is that death physical?

Master: Yes, you will enter the temporary state of apparent death.

Woman A: I have heard of this. There have been circumstances in the past where people have physically died during the meditative state. Is that possible, if you go into that state?

Master: In order to prevent this danger, a special energy is stored in the microcosm of the body. This energy is called *kundalini**. Even though the body and mind come to the state of death externally, through the power of *kundalini* they can be resurrected. It rarely happens, because *yogis* prepare for it by devoting long hours to training and practice. If such an experience should happen suddenly, it should be understood that it occurred as a result of practice done in the person's previous lives.

It is rather strange, though, that in order to obtain immortality, you must die.

Gerald: Dying in the mind?

Master: Yes, the death of the mind.

The Guru and the Disciple

Prajna: Shri Mahayogi, will you talk a little bit about the role of the *guru*?

Master: The literal meaning of "*guru*" is "the light that dispels darkness." Darkness is ignorance and attachments within the mind. The light is the inherent essence of us all. However, when the darkness is so deep that the light within cannot remove the darkness by itself, a light must shine from the outside. This is the reason for the existence of the *guru*.

Guru is the **Truth itself**. If the *guru* is not the Truth itself, he or she cannot be called "*guru*." Of course, the Truth is the very Truth that exists within each. The aim is simply to remove the darkness—ignorance—that lies in between. As soon as it is removed, the boundary between *guru* and disciple no longer exists. When two lights come together, do they appear as two? There is only one light.

Prajna: Can you speak also about the role of disciples?

Master (smiling, but intent): Disciples must study hard with sheer commitment. For certain, they must desire Truth earnestly. The world throws upon you many kinds of stimulations and attractions. But the disciple must have great determination to prevail over all temptations, and to stand alone in true independence [Awakening]—not to be battered by the god of death. The more you continue to practice and discipline yourself earnestly, the more your *dharma* is clarified.

(Kristin says that she is grateful to be reading the book Karma Yoga *by Swami Vivekananda, recommended to her by Shri Mahayogi.)*

Kristin: In the book, he emphasizes the importance of the path of work, just like the article that was read aloud tonight. But I am still disturbed by the same thing I asked you about before, the teaching that says, "this world is just a dream." If this world is just a dream, then why does it really matter at all what we do?

Master: The only person who can truly declare "This world is a dream" is the person who is awakened. You may perhaps have an idea that you are within a dream, but you don't know this for certain until you truly wake up. Even though you are in a dream, it is probably a good idea to follow the teachings of Truth. If you do this, perhaps you will wake up in a more pleasant manner. (*Attendees laugh.*)

Karuna: Sometimes I read various recommended books or other books. I can tell that the only way to process the thoughts that are being presented is with my mind, because clearly I am not yet awakened. But then, sometimes, I get the sense that I should not be reading because it hampers the process of discovery. There is a book by St. Teresa of Avila called The Interior Castle, and I can only read up to some pages before I start feeling like I should not really read it any more. Should I read more?

Master: "Understanding" and "becoming" are different things. Indeed, *Satori* will not be revealed to you only by reading. Scriptures or teachings are, so to speak, like maps. You may be instructed in the whereabouts of the destination, but you cannot find the path to the destination because, regardless of what the map says, reality is altogether different. If you progress diligently step by step, however, you will come to understand correctly the map indicated by the scriptures. What is necessary is to go faithfully and incessantly toward the Truth with all your heart, mind and strength.

Woman B: Can one practice *bhakti yoga* within any occupation?

Master (smiling): It's possible. It does not matter what occupation one pursues as long as it is not illegal. (*All laugh.*) *Bhakti yoga* is just like thinking about your beloved all the time. It is probably more important than work, wouldn't you agree? However, you must work. (*more laughter*) So do your best with your mind and body at work, but allow your heart to think of your most beloved—God.

Alberto: We talked about *bhakti yoga* and *karma yoga*. Does one choose one and stick with it? Or is the practice to combine them?

Master: In the beginning, the form of the objects [of devotion] in these two paths may appear to be different. *Bhakti yoga* is devotion to God—thinking of your ideal God—and *karma yoga* is to serve with devotion all others in the world. However, if it is understood that all things are nothing but different forms of the beloved divine, then *karma yoga* and *bhakti yoga* become one path.

Alberto: Do you decide [the path] for yourself? I have a preference.

Master: These two do not contradict each other, so go forward from where you find ease of practice.

Alberto: So then it is like a car that brings you somewhere. (*All laugh.*)

Master: Everything is God; there is only *Atman*, so you will realize that the car too is God.

Kundalini

Scott: In our *asana* practice, there is a high concentration of *asanas* that focus on the third *chakra*. Could you please discuss the significance of this *chakra* regarding the circulation of *prana* and the activation of *kundalini*?

Master: The power that moves the entire universe, including the mind and body, is *prana*. This *prana* is divided into five functions within the microcosm: *prana* [as a *vayu**], which conducts respiration from the nose to the heart; *samana**, which conducts digestion from the heart to the navel; *apana**, which conducts excretion from the navel down; *udana**, which conducts the ascension of energy from the nose upwards, activated when the body dies or is in the state of deep meditation; and *vyana**, which conducts regulation over the entire body.

The third *chakra* is called *manipura chakra**, and it is the center of *samana*. Its main physiological function is to digest food. It has the quality of fire within the subtle body. *Kundalini* is located below it. [Thus, with practice,] *apana* and *prana* are unified at *samana*; *samana* then increases the heat of the united energy. This heat gradually begins to awaken and to raise *kundalini*. This is the close relationship between *samana*, the *manipura chakra*, and *kundalini*.

To be sure, the *asanas* that we practice do not concentrate only here at this point, though it is a fact that the system of Yoga is based on the principle of fire. In the time before Yoga, that principle was called *tapas*, which means heat. Long ago, there were ascetics who tried to generate heat [through the practice of asceticism] by mortifying their flesh. However, this proved ineffective because they still had the desire for happiness in the next life. The appearance of Yoga changed the purpose of practice from desiring benefits in the afterlife to desiring realization of the Truth. From this point on, the meaning of "heat" started to change from external stimuli to internal purification. This is the system that constitutes Yoga, as well as the practice that Buddha underwent.

Egil: During a recent fast, I noticed the body getting a little cooler sometimes and the digestive fire weakening a little bit. Is this the same fire that Yoga practices work on?

Master (speaking definitively): In Yoga, fasting is not recommended. This is because, as you are experiencing now, when the fire of Yoga intensifies, it is capable of transforming into heat capable of destroying the body. Yoga is neither for those who eat too much, nor for those who perform fasts. Especially in *hatha yoga* or *kundalini yoga**, it is necessary to take in moderation the appropriate *sattvic** foods. The foods are consumed by *shakti** within the body or, in other words, *kundalini* eats them. Therefore, stop fasting immediately and gradually begin to eat *sattvic* foods. In general, it is said that fasting is effective for improving various illnesses and physical troubles. However, if you are already healthy it is not necessary.

(With his eyes fixed on Shri Mahayogi, Egil nods in understanding.)

Gerald: What are *sattvic* foods?

Master: A diet that is based on mainly vegetables.

(A woman in the front row who had been actively and eagerly asking Shri Mahayogi questions, poses another. She says she has been practicing meditation for five years, and speaks of the headaches she gets when she feels kundalini *rising. After a short pause, Shri Mahayogi asks her to explain in more detail.)*

Woman A: It begins at the perineum, the very base of the spine, and I can feel it moving in a circular motion. As it travels, there is a relaxation I feel in the body, almost like floating, floating with the arms, and I feel as though my whole body could float at that point in a very calm space, until I feel that the energy has completely gone through my limbs into my third eye, and that is when the tension arises.

Master: Analyzed accurately, that is the state before [the awakening of the] *kundalini*. The true ascent of *kundalini* goes through the *sushumna**, which is the central path in the spinal column. In order for the energy not to swerve into other parts, you must concentrate only on the *sushumna*. It is said that in the body there are 72,000 *nadis**, the paths through which *prana* flows. But with *kundalini*, only this single *sushumna* is important.

Perhaps real *kundalini* will eventually begin to rise. In your current situation, think of it this way: *kundalini* is *shakti*; *shakti* is a goddess. Therefore, concentrate upon that power and think of it as a goddess; that is, the element of *bhakti* is required here. Then, the goddess will help you to remove the various difficulties.

Woman A: Thank you.

Alberto: Mahayogi, it seems to me that desires attach themselves to the ego or the mind, and I would like to get rid of these desires or let them go. Could you say something about how one can find a way to let go? I always like to think that I'd like to surrender, not so much because of what I want but what God wants.

Master: In order to see what others want, you must have already eliminated your own desires. In order to eliminate your own desires, you must discern whether the desire is eternal or not—real or not.

Alberto: I don't understand that. What do you mean by "whether the desire is eternal or not"?

Master: If your mind or ego has attachments toward objects of the world, then once they disappear you will be able to feel what others want. Then you will be able to offer yourself [in service] to others.

Karuna: Are you saying that the object of desires must be eternal?

Master: Yes.

Priya: Mahayogi, several weeks ago I asked about serving people who are very sick, or dying. Among other things, you instructed me to smile always. Sometimes when I am with a person who is crying, I can smile, but I can cry with them, too. It seems to help. Am I doing anything that I ought not to be doing?

The next question is, when I'm smiling, I notice things happen depending on which eye I am watching with. Please say something about it.

Master: A soft smile is the best gift. However, it is also important to cry together according to the needs of persons and situations. Everything is done by the mind of compassion.

Regarding the difference between the right and left eyes, since ancient times it has been said that the god *Indha** (*Indra*) abides in the right eye. This has been recorded in ancient sacred scriptures, such as the Upanishads. That is the difference between the right and left eyes.

Priya: What about the other eye?

Master: According to this scripture, the right eye is the divine eye and the left eye is the human eye.

Priya: Is there a way to perceive this information while with someone?

Master: Well, perhaps if you try concentrating on the right eye, you might see God [*Purusha**].

Priya: Can Mahayogi say something about the mind of compassion?

Master: The mind of compassion is inherent to everyone. However, ego, desires and attachments hinder it from being activated. Because of the ego, there are "myself," "others" and diverse things; the ego-consciousness differentiates oneself from others. As the ego weakens, and eventually vanishes, the distinction between oneself and others disappears. Regardless of however many forms are manifest, in fact, there is only one thing—*Atman*, or God itself. That Self is you—you yourself are the one who is in front of you. If you see yourself suffering, how can you do other than to reach out and help yourself? There is no need to look for something in return. Just share the joy of bliss, simply with a smile (*smiling gently*).

(Seekers' questions continued without pause. They have been so concentrated on Shri Mahayogi that they seem to have lost the sense of time.)

Master: Today, because of your heightened enthusiasm, we have gone quite past the time. These enjoyable moments have passed quickly, and now we must go. There will be another *satsangha* in two weeks. I will see you then.

Satsangha (Kyoto)

IX

The Truth of all Beings

(Saturday, 17 September 2005, Kyoto)

Today's satsangha *has an international flavor, with several westerners in the* ashrama: *a visitor from New York; Brent from Oregon; Jacob (who found out about Mahayogi Yoga Mission through "Yoga Asanas"*), and his friend Randy, both from California. Jacob and Randy offer a mango and a bouquet of oncidium flowers to Shri Mahayogi. They sit beside Vishoka, the translator of the* satsangha. *Over thirty people are assembled, eager to begin.*

The Path of Yoga and the Path of Karma

Endo: I like the expression "to live in the moment." I strive to do it, but I notice that sometimes I travel back in time to my past feelings, or to my worries about the future. Please teach me why it seems impossible to focus on the present, and how it is possible to live moment to moment.

Master: Our bodies and minds are compelled to remain active. It has become so habitual that it is almost instinctive; it's quite difficult to stop for even a very short while. If the mind remains still for even an instant, immediately it recalls memories from the past and becomes anxious about the future. From a psychological point of view, you can say that the mind brings about the relationship of attachment in the form of memories. This implies that by cutting attachments, binding memories are released from the mind. If "instinct" is the result of habitual action, it is also possible that stillness can result from habitual action.

In the system of Yoga, practice of *asanas* stills the body, whose nature is constantly active. This in turn stills the breath, which accompanies the activities of the body. Furthermore, by learning the Truth and practicing meditation, one can remove attachment and ignorance. Through this discipline, the mind's agitation stops. Mastery comes only through training. Practice, practice, practice.

(A few people smile wryly while Shri Mahayogi laughs lightly.)

Endo: Besides practicing *asanas* and meditation for a certain number of hours per day, what else are we required to do practically in daily life?

Master: The main obstacles to training are illnesses, injuries, or anxiety and agitation of the mind. Regular practice is essential in order to treat these and prevent future occurrences. By intensifying the passion of your search for the Truth, true faith will come. Also, by deepening your practice of *bhakti yoga*, *karma yoga* and *jnana yoga*, you will outgrow all your daily problems. (*to Endo, who gives a wry smile*) Don't you think so?

Endo: I am sweating. (*Everybody laughs.*)

Visitor: Karma Yoga is the service of helping those who are suffering; *bhakti yoga* is devotion to God; and *jnana yoga* is discrimination upon what is real. But what is real? Your relationship with God, and everything else is not real? Is this right or...?

Master: If you are able to carry out your discrimination to that end, then you will realize that there is only Truth, or Reality. This is what is called "God," and is the Truth within yourself.

Visitor: So ultimately, you are a part of God, or you are God, or Truth, which means that you merge with that in *samadhi*?

Master: To say it more precisely, it is not being one "part" of God—it is being God itself. Nor does one "merge" with God—one awakens to the True Self. This Awakening is not the ultimate goal of Yoga only—it is the ultimate point of *all* religions. Why? Because Truth is only That! Experience it for yourself within *samadhi.*

Visitor: Is the soul's purpose to experience *samadhi*, achieve Awakening, and realize God?

Master: That's right.

Visitor: So everything that happens to me must be good for me, taking me in that direction, because whether positive or negative, everything that happens is going in that direction, correct?

Master (after a short of silence): All events can be classified in two ways: what is pleasant and what is painful—what is "good" and what is "bad." These are all relative things. There is an alternative: what is the Truth and what is not. Do you follow the words of Truth or do you ignore them? From this, the way of Yoga and the way of *karma* diverge. If you seek for the Truth, you must choose the path of Yoga.

Jacob: When we are in meditation or practicing Yoga, is it good for us to recall the Master, to think of Shri Mahayogi?

Master (smiling): Yes, indeed. Please practice this way. *(Apparently, Jacob has had a meeting with Shri Mahayogi once before. He confessed to his friend with a smile that he had "already met him in meditation.")*

The Truth of the Universe

Brent: Scientifically, there is an understanding that the universe was made fifteen billion years ago, the earth four and a half or five billion years ago, and human beings were created much more recently. At a certain time, God said to Moses, "I am that I am," and *Brahma** said to Buddha, "Please teach people about Awakening," and then they began teaching people—all of which suggests that God existed and exists independent of human beings. I'm curious about the nature of God because, at least historically, it seems that God is quite independent of human beings and does not need human beings, as we are his creations. So then the question really is, I think, does God separate from us? Is to be united with God what we must do?

Master: The commonly held belief that God created the entire universe and all beings is something that does not exist in the East. Instead, in India, since the remote past, people have kept asking: What is God? There are lots of gods, but what is behind these gods, and what is the fundamental cause of all? What is this tremendous strength that manifests the universe, keeps nurturing all beings, and makes the universe move and keep moving? There were many seekers before Buddha, who inquired into these fundamental questions.

Much research was also done about the physical nature of the universe. It is true that from the point of view of modern science, it could appear that the universe started with "the big bang" at a certain moment, and then evolved into the present, and that this could represent, so to speak, a linear evolutionary path. However, if you look at the way of all life, it is clear that life repeats cyclically—it appears, then perishes. There is no other system whatsoever in this entire universe. Even the universe was born at a certain point and will also eventually perish, or disappear. In the remote past, which we cannot even imagine with our minds, the same process and the same things must have recurred again and again, and they will repeat themselves into the future. From the point of view of Indian thought, evolution is not linear, but a cyclical spiral.

There is a sacred scripture in which Krishna* utters the words, "No one can know the beginning and the end; humankind can only know the middle."

This means that the cycles are repeated eternally. This profound wisdom is a result of the fervent quest for the Truth in India, and also represents the core of Yoga.

Upon close observation of our daily life, three main patterns emerge: the waking or conscious state; then, the dream state, which is a completely different realm from the conscious state, but in which dreams seem real; and thirdly, the state of deep sleep, which is experienced daily, and in which dreams are not even seen. All sufferings and hopes arise in the waking state. From where do they come? From experiences. Even twins have different mental worlds, so the world of experiences does not mean only the experiences in this life, but implies those of past lives as well. All of these things can be understood in terms of causality; everything has a cause and an effect.

The issue is **who the "I" is,** the central figure. There is a fourth state of consciousness that knows these other three states. This fourth state of consciousness is the state that is uninvolved with all movements of the mind. It is the Consciousness that simply sees, or knows all other states of consciousness, like a light. Usually, however, the ego, which prominently abides in the first state of consciousness, pretends to be this fourth state of consciousness [the ego pretends to be "I"]. Therefore, it is extremely important that we illuminate the true nature of "**I**."

Those who have realized the Truth, by relying on the important key words just mentioned, have appeared in an unbroken line throughout India. The testimony of what they realized is as follows: "What exists behind the entire macrocosm, sought for as the great Existence since ancient times, and the Existence within the microcosm, called the True Self or Truth, are one and the same." This Truth is unreachable by any word, and has no form. Even the word "God" cannot reach it. The only thing that can be said about it is simply: it **exists.** If you understand correctly the words from the Bible you quoted, they express it quite closely ["I am that I am"]. Only *that* is Reality. *That* is yourself.

The Truth is already within us. But it is just like this (*covering the mango beside his foot with his hands*) the mind covers and interferes with the Truth. Ignorance, or darkness, is the cover. Therefore (*blowing on the mango and removing his hands*), you have to get rid of it. By doing so, the Truth that is already within, will shine by itself.

Ambika: Many religions, especially some institutions of Christianity and present-day Buddhism, like Brent mentioned, teach that human beings were created by God, and that we humans are sinful, and must purify our sins. I am wondering if it was not a direct revelation by Moses or Buddha, but something that was introduced later, by churches or others for the purpose of making the teachings easier for children to understand.

Master: The Truth is universal, and is so even for children. Like the sun that shines onto every corner of the world, Truth has no differentiation. If there is a religion that claims that only they are right and others are wrong, or if there is a religion that teaches, "Our religion is the only way to salvation," one can frankly say that they are mistaken.

Many people cling to religion out of desperation to escape pain and sorrow, or in hope of salvation. It is like clutching at straws. They need immediate relief. Throughout the world, there are many [religious] teachings, which are used as a means to provide that temporary relief by offering salvation. However, if a religion attempts to keep people further bound to it, it is a mistake on the part of the religion. In the same way that you learn worldly things at school—going through elementary, middle, high school, and then proceeding to a specialty institution—you have to proceed beyond the lower grades to the higher grades in religion. Until one reaches the ultimate level of Truth, suffering is not completely resolved.

Truth is completely autonomous. It exists by and of itself, with no reliance on any other thing—no dogma, religion, history, institutions, nor any other authority whatsoever. Such pure and noble existence is the Truth of our very selves—of all beings and the universe.

Looking at the grand scale of time, the past two thousand years of history are only a brief, barely visible flash. However, in this brief period countless cruel acts have been committed, and are still being committed, in the name of religion. It can be understood as a reflection of ignorance in the human mind, or religious ignorance.

The Truth cannot be monopolized by anybody, nor by any religion.

Release From the Cycle of Reincarnation

Brent: Could you speak to us a little bit about the nature of our existence between incarnations?

Master: Reincarnation can be described as one individual mind having to act out its *karma* through numerous existences. If you have done good, consequently you will receive good results; if you have done bad, you will receive bad results. If you have not yet exhausted the desires in your mind, the objects of attachment, then you must be born again in order to fulfill them in another life. This is the way it goes, from the past to the present existence, and from the present existence to the next.

What then is the state between incarnations? You can understand reincarnation as being a reflection of the states of the mind or the result of the causes in your mind. Concerning the state in between reincarnations, actually, you experience a similar state every day, in the world of dream. Just as you wake up with the arrival of morning, the next life happens when the time comes. The events of our human life themselves signal the course of reincarnation. And the things you think about during the day are the content of your dreams, so you should always try to have good thoughts.

Ambika: I feel that the states of my mind—yesterday, today and tomorrow—are not really different from day to day. If I really dislike being stuck in the same state, should I take actions to cut off all my attachments during the waking time, so that I will be able to wake up the next morning in a different state?

Master: Yes. Yogic philosophy is very interesting. Philosophy is a way to understand many different things using symbolic equations. According to yogic philosophy, all things in this material universe are compelled into action by three different elements, or three qualities, called *gunas**. Even in a situation where the same thing appears to be happening continuously, if you look at the fine details as if with a microscope, you will actually see that the past and the present have the same conditions. The succession of one to the other is an illusion; the fact is they only *seem* to be continuous. Physically speaking, because the conditions of each moment are the same, our minds misconstrue them as continuous, one following the other.

This equation may be applied as follows. One notices something happening that one doesn't like. At that very moment, a gap is formed—the gap of "noticing." So it is possible in the next moment to bring about new action; to make a change in oneself. This is the yogic way to analyze, and to address and eliminate certain situations.

It is also true that there is a kind of force assigned to subconscious memory that functions as a deterrent to the breaking of this illusion of continuity. It is called *sanskara*. This is the very reason why one has to always accumulate good *sanskaras*. Using the same equation I just mentioned, you must choose to bring in the *sanskaras* of Yoga, not the ones of *karma*. Yoga means Truth. Faith, too, is a great help for this purpose.

Hodono: Some time ago, when Ambika asked a question about the meaning of the descent of an *avatara**into the world, Shri Mahayogi said, "Enjoy the taste of the blessing and then spread it to the whole world." And then, "But, you must not coddle the mind." Please teach me about this.

Master: What I meant was that if you coddle the mind, the mind creates ignorance using the ego, so you should avoid this. You need to use the mind to be active in the world, but you have to realize that the mind is not the protagonist. The protagonist is the *Atman*, which is the fourth consciousness, or the True Self. The mind is a servant, a subject or an instrument of the true master. Therefore, you must not indulge the mind. Only then will you be truly able to play freely. This is *lila**. (*speaking to new attendees*) Lila is one of the great teachings of Yoga. Its meaning is that all things are the manifestation of God, and even though time may be finite, God, as the essence of all, is simply enjoying this play.

(*Shri Mahayogi's answer reminded us of the meditation scene in the theatrical play,* Amrita-Immortality *, wherein the disciples in their roles as various bodies of* shakti *each voice the following lines:*

Withdraw the senses into the mind.
Withdraw the mind into the intellect.
Withdraw the intellect into the Atman.
Realize the True Self.
From the vibration of Om, *everything emerges,*
and one life evolves into various shapes.

This has been described as Shri Mahayogi's actual experience in meditation.)

Master: Truly, meditation is mystical and interesting! *(Shri Mahayogi laughs as if exhilarated.)*

It reveals so many things that are usually invisible, and what is impossible to understand becomes possible. And when the meditating mind is released from the body, you can experience union with the universe, or going to the moon—any kind of thing is possible! *(laughing)* And yet, these are still something similar to a world of "dream." Beyond this mysterious world, the Truth *is*. All of what you do by learning and meditating is only for you to awaken to the Truth.

Brent: Some say that without training you should not meditate on your own, or without someone who can guide you. Without instruction, it is best not to try to do it.

Master (decisively): You do not need to be concerned about it anymore because you have arrived at a true guide.

(Brent seemed unable to conceal his happiness, and continued his question.)

Brent: Some people want to attain salvation, some people try to attain Awakening. Shri Mahayogi spoke about the *Eightfold Right Path**, and that anybody can attain Awakening by following this teaching. Now, what is the difference between those who are struggling to attain this condition and those who have achieved it?

Master: Really, who is it that is saved? We cannot say that it is the Truth which is saved, because Truth never needs saving. That which is "saved" is the mind.

The mind is always looking for happiness. When the mind encounters some small happiness in this life, it seeks to redouble that happiness. This desire to multiply happiness continues unceasingly, eventually resulting in a suffering that crushes the mind. And then, the mind begins looking for "salvation."

Yoga, or the Truth, simply teaches that happiness does not exist on the outside; it is further within the mind, in a deeper region. In this world all things have their limit. The mind, however, does not understand this. This is the mistake of ignorance. Truth teaches us very simply that there is not a single thing in this world to which it is worth forming attachment. At the same time, if the mind really looks for salvation, it will eventually look for the Truth. This is because Truth is Eternal Bliss, which can never be broken. Those who are on the way are called "struggling." Those who have fully realized the Truth, they simply *exist.* You can never be sure of the difference by appearances— they might be your neighbors. (*laughing*) Even the very person himself or herself might not know it.

There is a hint here: if one is in the state of Truth, one is no longer unsettled by anything, and all suffering has disappeared. Furthermore, since there is no longer an ego, all actions are expressions of compassion and service for others. If you come across such a one, you simply and naturally feel like prostrating before that person.

So all you need is to strive! (*Everybody laughs.*)

Tomorrow will be the harvest moon, which in Japan is said to be the night of the year when the moon is the most beautiful. Traditionally, people offer special sweet dumplings to an altar and enjoy looking at the moon.

(*Shri Mahayogi speaks to the foreign attendees.*) Well then, have a good time here.

(*All prostrate themselves before the Master.*)

Satsangha *ends in an intense and bright atmosphere.*

X

Divine Play

(Saturday, 3 December 2005, Kyoto)

It is the last satsangha *in Kyoto of 2005, just before Shri Mahayogi departs for his visit to New York. The ashrama is filled with new attendees and many disciples, some of whom have traveled great distances to be here.*

The questions and answers in the first half of the session focus on the subtle body and kundalini. *In Yoga, the subtle body is purified by activating* kundalini, *the primary source of heat and tremendous spiritual power, which enables us to attain the invisible Truth.*

Shri Mahayogi teaches that in order to purify the sushumna, *the channel through which the* kundalini *rises, and enable* kundalini *to travel up through it, one must have a foundation of diligent practice and study, then apply the heat that arises from concentration and* kumbhaka*. *Psychological purification, including the removal of* kleshas *and attachments, also plays an important role in the process. Finally, the blessing of the divine* guru *is essential. Shri Mahayogi concludes by saying, "Passion in the quest for Truth and its realization—that is of the utmost importance."*

The Meaning of Life and the Search for the Self

(Takahashi, who has been visiting Shri Mahayogi frequently with his daughter for about a month, has brought his elder son, Noriyasu, who is in the midst of preparing for his university entrance exams.)

Takahashi: I brought my son here today because I wish for him to have the opportunity to experience this kind of atmosphere even for a brief moment because, exactly as you have just mentioned, passion for Truth is of the utmost importance. Is there a different way to explain or express this passion for Truth to young men around twenty years old?

Master: Well, I assume that this is something all of us have wondered about more than once from a very young age: **What are we living for?** Generally, people dream of having a nice job, working at it continuously and prospering until they die. However, many social structures have changed nowadays, and certainly people do not have a clear vision of their future health or of their lifespan. It is not tomorrow, or in the distant future, but perhaps at a moment's notice that people can get hurt in an accident. Conversely, even if people acquire through their work more wealth than they could possibly spend in a lifetime, would that make them feel happy?

To ask what one is living for is, after all, to inquire into **the existence of one's own Self.** If you think that your job is everything, then you are nothing but a slave to your job. If you think that money is everything, this means that you have become a slave to money. If you think that gaining power is everything, this indicates that you are a slave to power.

What is the True Self? The closest "I," or one's Self, is the biggest mystery for everyone. The mind may be carried away by various events in the world, but who is the protagonist of the mind? The answer to this is known as **Truth**. The Truth is nothing but Reality. Look around you to see whether there is Truth in the world. There is a word that has been used since ancient times—"God." What is God? This is also a question that must be resolved.

After all, the central questions everyone asks are, "Who am I?" "What is Truth?" or "What is God?" It does not matter by which subject you begin your inquiry, but if you delve seriously into your search, you will eventually arrive at one of these three questions. But that is just the beginning. Only then does the real study begin: the quest of the Self to find itself.

(The room falls silent for a while.)

The quest to find the True Self—inquiry into *Atman*, or *Brahman*—has been central to Yoga since ancient times. At the same time, there has been exploration into why the True Self—our blessed and brilliant Existence— is forgotten.

The teachings of Buddha and Yoga have much in common. In this world, sickness, aging and death are inevitable. There is no one who can avoid them. And when one thinks about this, fear and suffering emerge.

What is the cause for all this suffering? Obviously, it is being born. Whatever is born must eventually die. But there must be a cause for birth. When you continue to analyze it in this manner, in the final analysis, you will come to the conclusion that the cause is attachment to the world. This is commonly referred to as *karma*. Once one has desires or thoughts, they will not disappear until their actualization. If you die before they are actualized, they will remain, and will be prepared to be fulfilled by their actualization in a future lifetime, meaning that you will be reborn into another body.

It is important to understand the cause of *karma*. Ignorance—the error of looking for eternity and joy in the world without knowing the Truth—is the fundamental cause. The 108* or more *kleshas* ensue, and one becomes attached and enslaved by them, consequently increasing *karma*. All of this results in pain and suffering. Supposedly the mind desires happiness, but this apparent happiness soon metamorphoses, revealing a form that is ugly.

To ask what we are living for is to inquire into the Self thoroughly and earnestly. This is the process that will eventually lead you to the Truth.

Takahashi: Thank you very much.

(Noriyasu is listening quietly all the while. The powerful words of Truth fill the ashrama, *inspiring not only Noriyasu, but also the hearts of everyone present.)*

(Knowing this is the last satsangha *before Shri Mahayogi's departure to New York, some disciples wish to dedicate one last offering, an encore of the* kirtan*, "Dina Dayala Hari*."*

Inoue, sitting in front of Shri Mahayogi, explains the contents of the song. Accompanied by the rhythm and sounds of the tabla and other instruments, the joyful, uplifting singing of the disciples rings through the ashrama.*)*

Hari*, compassionate to the poor,
the most compassionate Hari
Radha's* beloved Hari, Govinda* Gopala*
His sweetness steals my heart, Krishna Gopala
Radha's beloved Hari, Govinda Gopala
Mirabai's* lord, powerful upholder of Mountains
The most precious jewel of Vrindavan*, Gopala

Masa: All of these terrible worldly events have been happening in rapid succession and society is losing its balance. Since this universe is created by thoughts, I wonder if those who aspire to become *yogis* can constantly deepen their thoughts on Truth to create a tremendous energy of true benefit to the world. If one person attains Awakening, this will help balance the thoughts of the world, correct? In this sense, is it correct to assume that if one has the chance to come in contact with Shri Mahayogi, one can get uplifted, and can then contribute to restoring balance in the world?

Master: That is so. There are many ways to help others. For those who are suffering from starvation before your very eyes, you can give bread. In less than three days time, however, they will suffer from hunger again, and then you must give again. What else can we give besides food? For instance, by giving knowledge, skills or education to those that are suffering, you can enable them to find work and earn money for food to live for months or years. However, even this is not absolute stability.

Spiritual blessings can give supreme happiness. They can bring endless bliss—not only in this life, but eternally.

If you look at society, you can see many different forms of aid being given. There are needs that must be dealt with urgently, as you mentioned—bare necessities are needed, such as food to survive, clothing and shelter for protection from the elements. Unbeknown to us, however, are people who are absorbed in the state of Yoga, deep inside mountains and caves. In India, this way has actually been honored for some thousands of years. Their vibrations of bliss have been emanating uninterrupted for the happiness and benefit of humanity for thousands of years, transcending time, and constantly benefiting not only humans, but all sentient beings in the universe.

May you take action to help others constantly, starting with what is right in front of you. May you deepen in Yoga, get closer to Awakening and become an existence that is truly righteous.

As I always say, artisans know their tools; so does God know where the great tools are available, and each tool is used according to need. What an individual can do then is sharpen oneself in order to become a better tool.

The honor is not intrinsic to the tool. All honors must be given to God, who is nothing but the True Self—everyone's Reality. This is the Truth.

(Silence prevails again.)

Our World as the Divine Play

Wada: Hearing the teaching, "Live in the world as if you are an actor on stage," I initially interpreted it as the ability to see oneself objectively, in the depth of suffering, as one acting out a role.

Shri Mahayogi says, "God simply wants to be entertained." I can enjoy the play of God when I am having a good time, but when I am having a hard time or feeling sad, I can't comprehend it in terms of God simply wanting "to be entertained." Please explain to me in easy-to-understand language what motivation I should have when I act out my roles.

Master: It is often said, "Life is a stage." Certainly, as the program changes, so the lines and attire often change. However, it is only one same actor or actress who is always performing. Life is just like this—you are playing many different parts. At one time you are a child, at another time you are a student, girl, lover, father, mother, many different professions, etc. (*smiling*) Nevertheless, there is only one person that is going through all of these. Even your name changes according to your role.

So then, what is the real substance? What is the true character of a human being? If you delve further into this inquiry, you must eventually ask the ultimate question: What is *Atman*? Or what is God?

Lila, the teaching in Yoga that the world is the [divine] play and sport of God, cannot be compared to the plays written by playwrights. In this world, various roles are meted out, and various dramas are developed. Nonetheless, their essence is *Atman*—God. So then why does *Atman*, or God, who is flawless and ever free, manifest into different forms? That is the secret of *lila*: its only purpose is to be enjoyed.

If you see this world with the mind, it appears as complex, marked by differences, and full of contradictions. However, if you see it with the eye of *Atman*, removing all names and forms, there is only *Atman*. *Atman* is playing for the sake of joy. This is *lila*. The word "*lila*" derives from a word meaning "the glancing light emitted by sparks —a flash."

(Shri Mahayogi smiles and addresses everyone.)

Master (looking at Wada): Do you know what joy is?

Wada: Joy? What is it...to be with Shri Mahayogi? *(Everybody laughs.)*

Master: If it were so, is that the only way you can be happy?

Miyatake: Is it to be absorbed in something, totally forgetting one's own self?

Master: That is still within the bounds of a hobby.

(Hearing the answers, some mumble and some laugh. Everyone is puzzled.)

Takahashi: Is it to act without attachment?

Master: That is irrelevant. *(Shri Mahayogi laughs.)*

Wada: I will say again, to be with God?

Master: What if we were to change the word "joy" into something similar, like "bliss"?

Wada: To return to the essence?

Takagi: To become free?

Master: That is true, but remember, we are talking about *lila*.

This world is tricky, really. For instance, just as reincarnation is symbolized by the cycle of a day—from waking up in the morning, to going to sleep at night, to dreaming—enjoyment and joy are hidden within daily life.

In what activities do you get most engrossed? What is it that causes you to feel free and forget about yourself and your attachments?

Wada: Practicing Yoga?

Master (conclusively): It's love, isn't it? When you see your loved one joyous, isn't it your joy? Surely there is nothing higher than that.

So, how can you experience the joy of others? How?

Miyatake: To be one...isn't it?

Master: No, it has to be more concrete.

Ambika: By serving that person in the way that makes her happy.

Master: That is correct. To give yourself. It is so simple (*laughs*).

Love each other, and give to each other. Then there is only bliss, there is only joy.

Shachi: If one feels that one does not have the means to serve, what should one do?

Master: That is impossible. Everyone has the means. It is unnecessary to feel this way. That is ignorance.

Takagi: So then, where is the clue hidden?

Master (smiling): Everywhere.

Sananda: Shri Mahayogi, you mention that you will

be happy when a disciple becomes awakened. Is this what a disciple can offer to the *guru*?

Master: Indeed. Awakening does not mean to be still and do nothing. Awakening makes one do nothing but serve and be loving and compassionate to all. That is the essence of *lila*: to serve and give oneself.

Sananda: I have read a little about the life of Chaitanya*. There is a part that mentions that the *gopis'** love for Krishna is to want only Krishna's happiness. Even though they do not desire their own happiness or even a trace of their own joy, bliss inevitably comes. This bliss is so enormous that it comes without their seeking it.

(Shri Mahayogi listens, nodding his head in agreement.)

Sananda (continuing): When Radha and Krishna played together in the Vrindavan forest, the joy Radha felt was thousands of times more intense than Krishna's. Since Krishna cannot see his beautiful, supreme form by himself, in order to experience the joy that Radha felt, he incarnates again and again to play with his *bhaktas**.

Master: How exquisitely sweet that is! Indeed, we have forgotten how sweet the nature of *lila* is.

Kinkara: So then God's *lila* means God loves us more than anything else...and to love means to serve. In other words, God is giving love to us in the form of our ability to serve.

Master: Yes. That is exactly so.

Umeda: Does "to internally deepen *bhakti* and externally deepen *karma yoga*" mean that one cannot help serving because of love? In other words, the more love deepens, the more service follows spontaneously?

119

Master: Yes, that is so.

Miyatake: Although there are various forms, does this mean that it is unnecessary to guard oneself against other people? Rather, one should [ignore the external and] single-mindedly try to see the internal *Atman* in others?

Master: Yes. It is to see *Atman* through the *Atman.*

Takahashi: In the state where the feeling of love or service has not yet arisen, is it important to actively practice *karma yoga?*

Master: Yes, it is very important. The duties you are fulfilling—your job, providing for your family, societal responsibilities—are obligations, so these are considered passive *karma yoga.* Active *karma yoga* is to serve others in an even more unselfish way. Exert effort to practice the more active form of *karma yoga.*

It is also important to deepen *bhakti yoga.* As seen from our discussion of the essence of *lila,* these two [*karma yoga* and *bhakti yoga*] are not different from one another.

Eventually you will come to understand that what you refer to as *raja yoga, jnana yoga, bhakti yoga,* and *karma yoga*—this yoga and that yoga—are simply intellectual classifications, and that the spotless and absolute True Reality alone exists as Yoga, which is the crystallized essence of Truth.

(Shri Mahayogi's loving gaze gently engulfs the ashrama.*)*

To offer oneself and to simply love—this pure and noble love constitutes the essence of lila. *In unmistakable ways, we have been blessed with the opportunities to learn the ultimate dimension of this love.*

XI

Supreme Love

(Saturday, 3 June 2000, Kyoto)

The Five Attitudes of Loving God

(Sananda asks Shri Mahayogi about the actual way to practice bhakti yoga.*)*

Master: Bhakti yoga is also known as the yoga of love. Love is one of our inherent and essential states. When love extends from the ego, it ends up in slavery. Love that arises from unselfishness, however, moves closer to universal True Love. Love is love, yet great is the difference between love of one's own self and love for others. That is why *bhakti yoga* suggests that one find an object of pure love.

Just as one sometimes feels how dear the world is, so also one experiences, when the mind is at peace, how God dwells in all. This is called *shanta**, the disposition of peacefulness within the mind.

Furthermore, one loves God and desires to be loved by God. As the exchange of love fills the heart with contented bliss, one acts for God's sake, becoming his hands and feet. Seeing God as master, one serves Him. One enjoys an intimacy with God in this way. This enjoyment is not a worldly one. Tasting serenity and bliss, one yearns to be even more useful and devoted to God. This state is called *dasya**, which means "servant," but without any feudal characteristics. It is a service born out of love, as I just mentioned.

Though a slightly reserved attitude between "master" and "servant" remains in the state of *dasya*, if one gets closer, one becomes like a best friend. Best friends enjoy each other's company without a care about differences in education, etiquette, social status or power. There is no uncertainty. In family relationships, at work or in society, there are many social customs based on superiority and inferiority that can cause uneasiness. However, the relationships between best friends are built on equality, and pleasures and events are shared that lie beyond hierarchical boundaries. Communing with God through an open relationship is called *sakhya**, the friend-relationship.

There is another type of love, which is to see God as your own child; a tender infant. This is the unconditional love of a mother who nurses and gives her child anything it wants. It is an exemplary mother's love for her little child, never asking for anything in return. Hoping only for the child to grow in good health, she acts solely with warm affection. This is called *vatsalya**.

Then, there is self-oblivious love, wherein one is so madly in love that one forgets all else, like the crazed passion of lovers. This could well be the most intense love in the world, with the power to consume all. It is the love by which you would give even your own life for the sake of your lover, by any means and at any cost. You love simply for the sake of love. This love can be so intense that bliss and suffering become indistinguishable. There is only love and your lover, who dons love's form. *Bhakti yogis**, or *bhaktas*, love God this way—adoring, becoming mad for God, and then merging into God. God as formlessness manifests into form, appearing before the *bhakta*. Love itself is the most exalted emotion. The purer that love becomes, the more power love has to inspire unimaginable energy and spirit. Only then will you realize that **God is Love**.

The many events in the world to which we become attached are perhaps glimpses of love, or are in fact distorted appearances of love. In ancient Buddhism, the word for "love" and "attachment" is the same. Ordinary human love is often referred to as *raga** or *kama**. Both words also mean desire. The love of *bhakti*, however, is called *Prema**. It is pure, Supreme Love. The pure love of *Prema* lies within everyone. Unalloyed Love, *Prema*, is original, but when filtered through the mind, some of its tones change. Love itself is infinite, so regard love's various appearances in life as glimpses of *Prema*. In order to do so, through *bhakti*, burn with the longing for union with True Love—*Prema*.

For love, methods of study, practices and disciplines are unnecessary. (*smiling*) **Simply love**. That is enough. Just make this love grow stronger and stronger, and deeper and deeper.

Vivekananda described four paths of Yoga and left us with the famous phrase, "Do this…by one, or more, or all of these—and be free." In learning and realizing the Truth, *raja yoga*, *bhakti yoga*, *karma yoga* and *jnana yoga* are the same. Each one is a dynamic and efficient means. You could say that because *bhakti yoga* employs only the most immediate means, love, it holds tremendous power. God, Truth, longing for awakened beings and True Love is the *Satori* of *bhakti yoga*.

The Sweet Love of Krishna and Radha

Sananda: We all may have experienced the five dispositions of love, as Shri Mahayogi has just mentioned. Should we then understand that our love should be re-directed to God?

Master: Yes. Lastly, I would like to introduce a story that illustrates the five ways of *bhakti*.

Madhura*, which is the love of the lover, is strongly illustrated in the story of a young man, Krishna, who is an incarnation of God, and a *gopi*, a cowherd girl, in the Vrindavan Forest where Krishna spent his youth.

It is said that Krishna spent his childhood in the company of his foster mother, Yashoda, and with many friends on a farm, running in the forest with innocent abandon. He was loved by all the *gopis* who lived in the forest, and would often spend the entire night with them, singing and dancing. The woman who loved Krishna most deeply among the other *gopis* was called Radha. Krishna and Radha rapidly grew close, and the flames of their love ignited. But Krishna was a God-incarnate and often played with other *gopis* as well. One day Krishna left Radha for another *gopi*. A friend of Radha told her about it. Radha then wept. Swollen drops of tears fell from her eyes and she looked very sad. Her friend asked her, "Do you weep because your Krishna was stolen by another woman?" Radha answered, "No, that is not why I am crying. The tears come because I feel distress, knowing that my beloved Krishna will be displeased, because she does not know how to serve him."

In her sentiments, there are no feelings of jealousy, or anything. There is only the lover who, purely out of love, thinks only of service and devotion to her lover; so much so that if he is not treated properly, she is utterly distressed. This story may be just a myth, but it contains a wise lesson about love.

You can replace the God-incarnate Krishna with God, or *Atman* or *Brahman*. Or you can replace Krishna with the Truth. The story of Krishna and Radha teaches us *bhakti yoga*, and at the same time, it teaches us the ultimate ideal of *jnana yoga*, *raja yoga* and *karma yoga*. This is a great love story from which we have so much to learn. Stories of Krishna and Radha are often depicted in the forms of poetry, painting and other arts. Please keep in mind this exquisite, sweet love story.

XII

Guidance and Blessings

(Friday, 3 February 2006, New York City)
In the winter of 2005-2006, Shri Mahayogi again visits New York. This is the third satsangha *of his visit. There are 42 attendees. It begins with Kamalakshi's partial reading of the translation of a* satsangha *that took place on December 24, 2005 among disciples in Kyoto while Shri Mahayogi was in New York.*

The disciples in Kyoto have grown individually and as a sangha*. *They were unified and strengthened more than ever through their enthusiastic participation in last year's performance of Amrita-Immortality. The sangha's focus and energy continues even now. Amrita was successful not only as a creative event, but also as a demonstration of how each disciple's personal growth is the very blessing from the* guru. *It is a true spiritual treasure, wholly granted and promised to those who genuinely strive to the best of their ability, both internally and externally.*

America is the country of "individualism," but in order to realize the oneness of Yoga, one must deepen oneself, renouncing the mind's assertion of its individuality. Keeping harmony with others, one must proceed, seeing only Oneness. The experiences of disciples in Kyoto are shared through this reading, with the sincere hope of inspiring their brothers and sisters in New York. Hearing the experiences of fellow disciples can heighten our sense of responsibility and unity.

Kamalakshi's melodious and powerful reading draws in the hearts of the listening audience. As she reads, Shri Mahayogi gazes upon each one of the attendees, among whom are visitors from Japan.

Religions and the Truth

Prem: The text which was just read aloud spoke of practice in daily life, and how to communicate universally. I feel that as your students [and disciples] we must, at some point, be strong enough ourselves to communicate to people who don't have the opportunity to meet you or be in your presence. In daily life we meet different kinds of people—perhaps Christians, or people who aren't even consciously seeking anything, or worldly people. How do we communicate to these people in the same way that you communicate with us—without arguing, discussing, and without personal opinions? How do we communicate with people without letting our own personal opinions enter in?

Like Ramana Maharshi, in my experience with you, you communicate with me most eloquently through silence. How do we cultivate that presence, so we can communicate as clearly as you do?

Master: Always think, speak and act for the good of others. This is synonymous with the teaching, "Love thy neighbor." Truth is One. Without a word, it is conveyed, unfailingly, through silence. In coming into contact with various people in diverse situations, always act simply, solely filling your mind with what is best for the other person. Needless to say, in order to do so effortlessly, your own daily practice and self-training are required.

127

Lord Buddha was once asked by an unruly sort of man, still lacking in faith and understanding of the Truth, "What can I, a man like me, possibly do?"

Buddha replied, "Abstain from all evil, and perform good deeds."

Not only the Buddha, but all saints have taught this.

Kristin: Recently I spent some time in a Muslim country, and I thought I was going to live there. I was already your student at the time, but I found that I was not honest about that. I told people I was a Christian because I was embarrassed and I did not know how to explain Yoga. I feel confused about it. I feel ashamed that I could not be honest. I would like to ask you how can I explain Yoga and my religion?

Master: There are various religions in the world, but Truth in these religions, does it differ? No. Truth must be One. The difference is only in name. The view that, "only my religion is right and others are wrong," is a mistake.

The earth is one. The universe is one. If Truth is likened to a mountain, each path aims for the top of the mountain by its respective route. The actual summit is not visible on the way. This [inability to see the actual summit] indicates the incompleteness of religion.

Yoga knows there is only one summit: True Reality, without name or form. That Reality is all of us. Within that, there is no difference among religions.

The rivers that flow through the American continent, the rivers that flow through Europe, the rivers that flow through the Middle East, all flow into one ocean. At that point, does water argue about which river it came from? Have firm faith that the Truth is One, like the ocean. Religions must not be in conflict with one another, but in harmony. This can be realized by deepening yourself more and more; that is, by the realization of Truth, without a second. With unwavering faith, explain or talk to others about Yoga, Christianity or Islam.

Anjali: The reading today speaks about disciples' responsibilities. A large part of the responsibility that the *sangha* members in Kyoto speak of is their responsibility to each other in their practice; helping each other to continuously deepen their Yoga. How do we deeply understand the responsibility to *sangha*?

It seems every great being, including Shri Mahayogi, comes from a very unorthodox, and very non-traditional background and environment. They always have appeared alone, reforming what has come before them. With these kinds of beings as our greatest inspiration—quite individualistic, and apart from the group—how do we reconcile those two ideas in practicing as a *sangha*?

Master: Indeed, definitely the great ones have appeared alone. It has been proven throughout history.

When justice is weakened and vices prevail in the world, I manifest myself in order to preserve the good, destroy the wicked, and establish justice.

This is a well-known phrase from the Bhagavad Gita*. And certainly, the enlightened one's children come along. They are the disciples. The disciples follow the *guru*, and live the very way their *guru* lives. It is for the benefit of the disciples themselves, as well for all people, all beings and the entire universe. That is the order of the universe.

129

Guidance and Blessings

Man A: In practicing love and compassion for others, we may have people who are close to us for whom we have more love and compassion than we do for the people who are in our own families.

Sometimes this compassion for those who are closer to us might bring us further away from compassion to others who are not as close. How do you reconcile the two?

Master: Stop seeing differences between your family and others.

When Jesus was preaching at the home of a devotee, one of his disciples arrived with a woman. She said to Jesus, "Your mother is here." As soon as he saw the woman, Jesus said, "I do not know this woman." To him, whether it was his mother, who was a member of his family, or another woman, they were the same.

If you can, love your family or your lover as you love others; love others as your family or your lover. Love in this way.

Man B: Shri Mahayogi, along the same lines, speaking for myself, I have a close business relationship with somebody that I spend more time talking and dealing with than anyone else in my life. Many times this person can be very selfish, greedy and manipulative. On the one hand, I would like to find a place where I can be loving, compassionate and understanding towards him, and on the other hand, I find that I have to be a warrior, meaning I have to have very strong boundaries which I have to protect, and speak what I feel is the truth when I feel it is being violated. My *karma* is such that these people are intricately interwoven into the fabric of my life. Can you offer any words of wisdom?

Master: It really is a difficult issue. But, almost everyone in this society experiences similar problems.

Every action is *karma* and that is the truth. We are born into this life for a purpose, which is to extinguish *karma*. Needless to say, Yoga aims precisely at that. What, then, do people without the knowledge of Yoga do? Through various experiences, by letting *karma* take its own course, their *karma* is cleared, yet new *karma* is created again, and continues to accumulate. So, although interactions with people in diverse situations may be necessary, it is required that these interactions be controlled to a moderate amount and degree. And also remember that he, your business partner, may be experiencing his own *karma* in his own way.

So, you should not be bothered by such things any more. Concentrate only on deepening yourself.

Egil: It seems that in these modern times we have a very limited amount of time to do *asanas*. How can we ensure that we are practicing intensely within the limited time that we do have for the various *asanas*?

Master: Renounce all attachments and exclusively fill your mind with the perfection of Yoga—in other words, realization of the Truth. This does not mean to quit your job and do nothing. (*All laugh.*) Do your job diligently. You need to maintain your own body as well. The body is a vital vehicle for the completion of Yoga, but you do not need to be attached to the body any more than that. One third of a day can be spent for Yoga. Within that, *asanas* and meditation can be scheduled.

Egil: Concerning *karma yoga*, sometimes while practicing *karma yoga*, I try not to have any thoughts. Sometimes, however, I practice thinking "This is for God," and "the actions and the movements are for God," and also "God is performing the actions." Of these different modes, what is best?

Master: Any of them is fine.

Prajna: During meditation practice it seems that with the exhalation the mind sinks deeper, but then with the inhalation it seems to rise again. Do you have any advice for controlling this arising?

Master: In meditation, the breath bears a significant relationship. *Yogis* have discovered that there is a fourth breath apart from regular respiration. Plainly speaking, it is the state of no breath, or of nearly no breath. For instance, you may experience the sudden realization that you are not breathing while you are focused on something. As soon as you notice it, the breath comes in; then the concentration breaks. It can be said that all of our *asanas*, *pranayamas* and meditation in Yoga practice are to recondition the respiration. When these conditions are met comprehensively, meditation goes well. There is also another way through which this state occurs and that is forcefully through intense concentration. If you notice your concentration is about to break when the breath comes in, renew your concentration again.

Man C: Shri Mahayogi, you seem to use stillness like a tool, like something you can feel and touch and shape.

It seems like some sort of joyful attitude. For me, I find in approaching this attitude, it turns into sluggishness after awhile. So if you could, please say something to us about how to use stillness without becoming sluggish.

Master: Stillness is also called "peacefulness" or "bliss." This meaning has nothing to do with holding the body still. The issue is of the mind.

The mind is constantly disturbed by *karma* and the attachments caused by *kleshas*. The unbroken experience of this throughout many lifetimes may make you think this is quite normal. And, there may be happiness in these experiences, and suffering and grief also. What is the cause? It is the attachments of the mind. The Truth is simply that these are not your True Self. Your True Self is the Existence that is eternally still, peaceful and blissful.

If we learn what Yoga is, practice and discipline ourselves even a little bit, we must experience peace, if only for a brief or short moment. So, deepen your learning further, and improve your practices and disciplines. For certain, stillness or bliss will well up within you, and you will realize that *it is* your True Self.

Man D: I don't know anything about Yoga, but I just recently experienced the death of my father and I am not dealing with it very well. When I experience things like this, I usually isolate myself, and work through it on my own or with the pets I grew up with. But, I have experienced a lot of anger, and I worry for my mother because now I think that she is going to die. Living in New York City, I haven't had the opportunity to isolate myself. I am basically trying to find a way out, and I am just becoming more and more angry at everything and everyone around me.

Master: What are you angry at?

Man D: I don't know.

Master: Everything that is born must die eventually. There is no use in being angry about the way it is. But have no worries, because after this life people will carry on in another life. It is how people repeatedly incarnate. Why then must people reincarnate? The purpose is to reap what they have sowed themselves. This is the law of *karma.* Yet, there are people who live another way. They realize that there is neither freedom nor true independence in living bound to *karma,* and are determined to break out from it. The spiritual quest begins here; the teaching and the method is Yoga. If you learn unflaggingly, you will no longer feel fear in death. And you will not have anger.

The way to dissolve your anger is to study the Truth.

(Shri Mahayogi continues to gaze directly at the young man, an endless well-spring of compassion pouring through his eyes. It is as if the Lord Buddha himself is before us, speaking the Truth in a firm and gentle tone. It is said that all creatures and celestial beings bowed before the Lord Buddha. It must have been so, for witnessing this evening, one can feel all beings bestowed with renewed, exalted life.)

(Sahaja, who only arrived a short time ago, addresses the following question to the Master.)

Sahaja: Shri Mahayogi, I first met you about seven years ago. I remember it very well. When I came to see you, I said, "I don't believe that you are my master, but I believe that you can help me find him." And I asked you, "Would you help me?" And I remember you said nothing. I remember as I looked at you, you began to change. First, I saw a beast, then a few moments later, I saw the image of Christ; then I could not look at you any longer, Shri Mahayogi, and I turned away. And when I looked at you again, I said, "Will you be my master?" And again you said nothing, and again you began to change. This time, I saw just a golden disc floating in space. Again, I could not look any longer. I turned away, and when I looked back, I said, "What shall I do?" You said, "Return to your family and bring the love that you found into your home." And you said, "Return to your job and do it competently, no more, no less." And then you said, "Come and see me again sometime." So, I came to see you again.

Now, it has been seven years. And it has been hard—hard at work and at home. I am ready to leave home, and I have two young sons. What should I do?

(Although Shri Mahayogi nods warmly and listens, when Sahaja finishes speaking, he instantly appears serious. The Master fixes his direct gaze upon him and, in turn, Sahaja continues to gaze into Shri Mahayogi's eyes. The profound silence lasts for some time.)

(Sri Mahayogi eventually breaks the silence and speaks solemnly and clearly.)

Master: Your *karma* has been accomplished.[1] From now on, you must fully and seriously practice Yoga—that which is beyond *karma.*

(Shri Mahayogi's darshan continues upon Sahaja for a while longer. This may be the first time that such intense darshan is given in public. The atmosphere is heightened with a sacred charge; the surge of divine force is palpable and magnetic. Time and movement seem stilled.

Sahaja, his face aglow, joins his hands together as the most appropriate expression of respect and gratitude, and remains with his eyes closed for a while.)

Kristin: In *The Universal Gospel of Yoga,* you say, "Love for God can be sublimated to the point of madness." Can you say more about that?

Master: A holy being once said, "This world is like a mental hospital; you and I are all crazy. But my madness is better because I can see only God." Be That.

Ari: I, too, met you seven years ago at the *satsangha* in Chicago. At the time, I came to ask you a question because I was experiencing a lot of fear. I asked, "What do I do about this fear?" And you told me—not an answer to the question, it was something different—you told me, "You have to help people." I guess I've been trying to do that, and I feel a lot less fear now. When I recently heard you were coming, it was so important for me to meet you. I am here, and if there is something more I can do to help people, if you could give me some guidance, I would be so grateful.

Master (looking at her gently): First of all, I would like to say congratulations.

Do what you can with what is around you, and then gradually expand from there. To realize this, practice meditation consistently. That's all you need.

(Tears fall down her cheeks.)

Master: It was a very good *satsangha*. The time has come for today. I will see you in two weeks. Thank you.

From beginning to end, it is an energetic and potent satsangha. *Many feel from Shri Mahayogi the experience of something rare and special, where that which is beyond the five senses and intellect is made immediately present.*

Jai*
Satguru* Shri Mahayogi Paramahansa Ki* Jai
Om Tat Sat

---

1. The next day, when asked about the meaning of his answer to Sahaja ("Your *karma* has been accomplished"), Shri Mahayogi said:

   "The answer was appropriate for his present situation. Everything depends on whether or not he is determined to seriously, truly and fully practice Yoga from now on. If not, the *karma* that lies dormant will surface and claim power again."

   This answer reveals how Shri Mahayogi guides each of his disciples with encouragement and bold inspiration to step into the Truth.

Glossary

Entries in parentheses provide the alphabetical notation of the classical Sanskrit. In some cases, an entry may also provide the Hindi word as written in Roman letters.

108

In Buddhism, the word "klesha" sometimes means simply "worldly desire." It was often thought that these desires numbered up to 108. In Yoga, there are five fundamental kleshas, i.e. ignorance, egoism, greed, aversion and clinging to life.

Amrita (Amṛta)-Immortality

The title of a public performance organized by Mahayogi Yoga Mission on July 17, 2005, in Kyoto. This event had three parts: a play based upon the Katha Upanishad, one of India's sacred scriptures; a demonstration of the essential principles underlying the asanas; and a question/answer session.

The word "amrita" means immortality.

Ananda (Ānanda)

Supreme Bliss.

See "Sat-Chit-Ananda."

ananda (ānanda)

The feeling of joy or happiness derived from the Supreme Bliss of Ananda.

The characteristic of the fifth sheath of human beings.

See "five sheaths."

apana (apāna)

One of the five currents of prana (vital energy) in the human body. Apana works between the navel and the anus, and mainly controls the excretory and reproductive functions.

See "vayu."

asanas (āsana)

Originally, the sitting, or seated posture.

The two ways of sitting called siddhasana (posture of the

accomplished person) and padmasana (lotus posture) are regarded as the most important.

During the Middle Ages, various other physical postures were included in the asanas. As hatha yoga developed, the practice of asanas became established as an important method of using various postures to strengthen and purify the body, achieve control of the breath, and thereby attain tranquility in the mind.

ashrama (āśrama)
The hermitage where a sage dwells.
The place where practitioners engage in spiritual practice.

Atman (Ātman)
The real "I," or the "True Self."
The true nature of human beings, Pure Consciousness; the absolute existence that transcends self-identity or ego-consciousness.

avatara (avatāra)
A divine incarnation.
In India it is believed that the formless God adopts a human form and appears on the earth for the sake of awakening human beings to Truth.

Bhagavad Gita (Bhagavad-Gītā)
The holy scripture called "The Song of God," which is found in the great epic poem "Mahabharata." In this scripture, Krishna, an incarnation of God, teaches the Truth and the path of Yoga by preaching to General Arjuna.

bhakta (bhakta)
Lover of God.

bhakti (bhakti)
Pure love for God to the point of madness.

bhakti yoga (bhakti-yoga)
Yoga of love and devotion.
The path of Yoga that is at once the means and the end of union with God, love itself, through extremely fervent and intense devotion and service to God.

bhakti yogi (bhakti-yogin) (Hindi: bhakti-yogī)
A practitioner of bhakti yoga, a bhakta.

Bodhidharma (Bodhidharma)
The founder of Zen Buddhism.

bodhisattva (bodhisattva)
A seeker who works for the realization of Truth and the liberation of all life. Compelled by compassion and hope, a bodhisattva walks the path of self-sacrifice solely for the liberation of all beings rather than his or her own.

brahmin (brāhmaṇa)
A priest by inheritance of the highest order of the Indian caste system.

Brahma (Brahmā)
Personification of the universal Truth, or the highest god. Brahma is known in Japan as Bonten.

Brahman (Brahman)
The fundamental principle of the universe and the Absolute Reality.

Buddha (Buddha)
One awakened to the universal Truth.

This term also refers to a great enlightened being of ancient India. Buddha (463-383, 566-486, or 624-544 B.C.E.) was born into a royal family and lived without want or shortage. Realizing that everything in this world turns into suffering after all, he left his family and his palace to become a monk and renounced the world. After six years of the most severe ascetic practices, he meditated sitting under the Bodhi tree and finally awakened to the Universal Truth. He avoided any intellectual discussion and solely devoted himself to the salvation of people. He taught the four truths: suffering, its causes, the state without either one (Nirvana), and the eightfold right path toward Nirvana. He taught these according to individual circumstances.

Cave, The

The small space that has evolved into the local headquarters of Mahayogi Yoga Mission. Known as "The Cave," it is Shri Mahayogi's residence in New York.

Chaitanya (Caitanya)

(1486-1533)

A great bhakta (lover of God) born in Bengal in medieval India. His overflowing affection toward the Lord Krishna made him sing and dance insanely for the Lord and preach bhakti enthusiastically. He had an enormous influence on the development of a deeper understanding and transformation of bhakti yoga in India. To this day, Chaitanya is worshiped as an incarnation of God.

chakra (cakra)

Energy center inside the sushumna nadi that is physiologically related to nerve plexuses and psychologically related to spiritual states. There are seven important chakras: muladhara (at the end of the vertebral column-the coccyx); svadhishthana (at the sexual organ); manipura (at the navel); anahata (at the heart); vishuddha (at the throat); ajna (between the eyebrows), and sahasrara (at the top of the head).

darshan (darśana) (Hindi: darśan)

Blessing or grace. Literally, "seeing."
A saint's gaze is thought to bestow liberation. The guru's darshan accelerates the disciple's spiritual growth.

dasya (dāsya)

Servant.
One of the five bhakti attitudes toward God. In dasya, the bhakta sees God as his master and tries to get closer to God through wholehearted service.

Dharma (Dharma)

Truth.

dharma (dharma)

This word has various meanings. Among them are Truth, religion, justice, or duty.

Dina Dayala Hari (Dīna-Dayāla Hari)
"Hari, compassionate to the poor." The title of a kirtan
(a love song that entwines the soul with God).

Eightfold Right Path
The eightfold right practices that the Buddha taught for
the destruction of suffering and the realization of Nirvana:
(1) right view, (2) right thought, (3) right speech, (4) right
behavior, (5) right livelihood, (6) right effort, (7) right mindfulness
and (8) right samadhi.

First, one should learn the Truth and have the right view based
on Truth. Then, one can hold right thought. Speech and behavior,
rooted in right thought, also become right. At that point, one's
whole life becomes right (based on the Truth). In addition, if one
makes the right effort to keep the mind calm and practices right
mindfulness of the Truth, then the right state of samadhi
is realized. This samadhi destroys kleshas and karma, and it leads
to the destruction of any suffering caused by them.

five sheaths (kośa)
The five covers theory.
The teaching that describes human beings as composed of five
sheaths. These are the food sheath (physical body), the vital
sheath (prana body), the mental sheath (body of thoughts),
the intellectual sheath (body of knowledge) and the innermost,
blissful sheath (body of joy). The True Self, Atman, exists further
beyond the innermost sheath.
See "kosha."

Gopala (Gopāla)
One of the names of Krishna.

gopi (gopī)
Cowherd girl.
The sweet stories of love that unfolded between Krishna and
the gopis when Krishna was a boy represent God's supreme love
as it is conceived in bhakti yoga.

Govinda (Govinda)
One of the names of Krishna.

142

gunas (guṇa)

According to Sankhya philosophy, all phenomena in the universe are composed of three qualities or gunas: sattva (quality of purity), rajas (quality tending towards activity), and tamas (quality of darkness).

Sattva is essentially characterized by lightness and comfort, with a tendency towards brightness. Rajas is essentially characterized by stimulation and discomfort, with a tendency towards activity. Tamas is essentially characterized by dullness and heaviness, with a tendency towards stagnation that conceals everything. The loss of balance between these three components constantly creates instability and change in the universe. Moreover, tendencies in the human mind constantly undergo changes because of the gunas' influence. The practice and discipline of Yoga brings the mind and body to a sattvic condition.

guru (guru)

Literally, "the light that dispels darkness."
Master. "Satguru" means a true master who is awakened.
To fully realize Yoga, guidance from a guru is indispensable.

hansa (haṃsa)

Swan.
See also "paramahansa."

Hari (Hari)

One of the names of Krishna.

hatha yoga (haṭha-yoga)

The practice that is mainly focused upon the physical aspects of Yoga.
Hatha yoga is a step toward the goal of raja yoga. It consists of asana (posture), pranayama (control of the breath), mudra (sealing), and raja yoga (samadhi).

Indha or Indra (Indha or Indra)

An Indian god.
The most worshipped deity in India pre-dating ancient times.
The deification of the thunderbolt.
Indra is known in Japan as Taishakuten.

ishta (iṣṭa)
> The chosen ideal of God.
> A devotee's ideal or divine being that best represents perfection for him or her.

Ishvara (Īśvara)
> The personified form of God; the pure embodiment of Truth itself.

jai (Hindi: jay)
> Victory or glory.

Jai Satguru Shri Mahayogi Paramahansa Ki Jai
> "Glory be to Satguru Shri Mahayogi Paramahansa."
> Words of praise and faith in the Master.

jayanti (Hindi: jayantī)
> The holy celebration of the guru's birthday.

jnana yoga (jñāna-yoga)
> Yoga of knowledge.
> The path of Yoga that, through exhaustive discrimination of the True Reality (the True Self) from the unreal (the world), leads to Awakening to the True Self (Enlightenment).

kama (kāma)
> Desire.

karma (karma)
> Actions and their results.
> Selfish actions, or actions based on ignorance, bring about suffering; non-selfish actions, or actions based on Truth, bring about happiness. Because of these laws, the term "karma," together with its original meaning of "act," implicates the truth of causality and retribution.

karma yoga (karma-yoga)
> Yoga of action.
> The path of Yoga leading to perfect freedom—extinction of karma—and the consciousness of the Divine in all creatures, through detachment from the result of one's actions, fulfillment of one's duty, and devoted service to others.

karma yogi (karma-yogin) (Hindi: karma-yogī)
A practitioner of karma yoga.

ki (Hindi: kī)
A word used to indicate belonging or a possessive sense. For example: "Paramahansa Ki Jai" means "'Paramahansa's glory."

kirtan (kīrtana) (Hindi: kīrtan)
A love song that entwines the soul with God.

kosha (kośa)
Sheath.
Human beings are thought to be composed of five sheaths. See "five sheaths."

klesha (kleśa)
The fundamental cause of all desires, karma and suffering. There are five kleshas: ignorance, egoism, greed, aversion, and clinging to life. The foremost klesha, which generates the other four, is ignorance of Truth. Ignorance is seeing the non-eternal as eternal; seeing the impure as pure or perfect; seeing the painful as bliss; and seeing the non-self as Self.

Krishna (Kṛṣṇa)
A divine incarnation who lived in ancient India in about 8th to 10th century B.C.E.. His teachings in the Bhagavad Gita and sweet stories of love in Vrindavan make him the most beloved form of God in India, even today.

kriya (kriyā)
Actual practice.

kriya yoga (kriyā-yoga)
Yoga of practice.
The practice of Yoga comprised of three elements: tapas (austerity), svadhyaya (learning the Truth) and ishvarapranidhana (concentration on a divine being).

kumbhaka (kumbhaka)
Retention or cessation of the breath.
The natural occurrence of kumbhaka is the aim of pranayama, which is the practice of controlling prana by training the breath. It can also occur spontaneously during deep meditation.

kundalini (kuṇḍalinī)
An inexhaustible source of divine energy, which lies dormant within the human body in the muladhara chakra, according to Yoga physiology.

kundalini yoga (kuṇḍalinī-yoga)
The path of Yoga that seeks to awaken the sacred kundalini, the goddess in the muladhara chakra, and unite her with Shiva (Brahman), who abides in the sahasrara chakra. This is mainly practiced through hatha yoga.

lila (līlā)
An aspect of Truth: the world as the divine play of the One, God. By mistaking the mind for the master and forming attachments to the world with selfish thoughts, one experiences suffering. However, from the viewpoint of realization of the True Self, to the one who breaks this illusion (maya), the world appears as various forms of the one Existence, the One—God, playing by Itself.

madhura (madhura)
Lover.
One of the five bhakti attitudes toward God. In madhura, the bhakta gives God her most powerful emotion: Love for the lover. Blinded by the purest and most intense love, her mind becomes crazed and oblivious to all else, surrendering herself entirely to the beloved, God.

maharshi (maharṣi)
Great sage.
An honorific title for saints.

mahayogi (mahāyogin) (Hindi: mahāyogī)
Great yogi.

manipura chakra (maṇipūra-cakra)
The chakra at the navel.

mantra (mantra)
Sacred words, sounds or syllables repeated to assist concentration.

mantra yoga (mantra-yoga)
A method of calming the mind by chanting a mantra.

maya (māyā)
Divine illusion.
The mysterious divine power that conceals the monistic Truth of the one Reality (Brahman), creating the illusion of a dualistic world.

Mirabai (Mīrābāī)
(1498-1547)
A great bhakta (lover of God) born in Rajasthan in medieval India. From her very childhood, she only regarded herself as the lover of Lord Krishna. She left many poems describing her love for Krishna, which deeply move people not only in India but around the world even today.

nadi (nāḍī)
A channel in the subtle body through which prana (vital energy) flows.

Nirvana (Nirvāṇa)
The state of Satori (Awakening, realization of Truth). In this state, egoism is extinguished *like a candle blown out by the wind.*

Nirvikalpa Samadhi (Nirvikalpa-Samādhi)
The state of complete absorption without any cognition.
The state of Satori (Awakening), in which the mind disappears, and absolute, imperishable existence or consciousness is realized.

Om (Oṃ)
The divine syllable expressing True Reality, Brahman, or God.
The vibration or initial movement that constitutes the source of the universe. Om blends the three primordial sounds–"a," "u," and "m."

Om Tat Sat (Oṃ Tat Sat)
"God is True Reality."
The word Om expresses "God." Tat means "That." Sat expresses "True Reality."

paramahansa (paramahaṃsa)
Supreme swan.
Honorific title for great saints.

"Hansa" means a swan and "paramahansa" means the supreme swan. Swans can drink just the milk even when it is mixed with water, so its name is given to saints who see only the Truth in the world.

Paramahaṃsa (Paramahaṃsa)
Mahayogi Yoga Mission's bi-monthly Japanese newsletter published in Kyoto, Japan. It features the teachings of Shri Mahayogi and the experiences of his disciples.

prana (prāṇa)
The fundamental vital energy sustaining the universe and the driving force behind all of nature.
Prana manifests as the vital energy in the human body, and causes both the body's physical and mental functions and activities.

As a "vayu," prana also refers to one of five currents of prana (vital energy) in the human body. Prana works between the nose and the heart and governs the respiratory function.
See "vayu."

pranayama (prāṇāyāma)
Control of prana.
The practice of controlling prana through training of the breath, ultimately leading to control of the mind. The practice purifies the subtle body and prepares the mind for meditation. One of the disciplines in raja yoga.

Pranava Sara (Praṇava-Sāra)
The gospel of Satguru Shri Mahayogi Paramahansa, journalized in New York City between 1997-1998. Pranava Sara depicts Shri Mahayogi's darshan, sara (essence) of the pranava (words of Truth), and his ways and method of teaching according to the disciple's karmic station, level of spiritual development and personal circumstances.

pratyahara (pratyāhāra)
Control of the senses.
The practice of withdrawing the five senses so that they make no contact with external objects. One of the disciplines in raja yoga.

precept [of Yoga]
The precepts for yogis are: yama, which involves control of one's actions, words, and thoughts in relation to others; and niyama, which involves discipline of one's actions, words, and thoughts in relation to one's self.

Yama consists of ahinsa (non-violence), satya (truthfulness), asteya (non-stealing), brahmacarya (continence) and aparigraha (non-greed).

Niyama is composed of shaucha (purity), santosha (contentment), tapas (austerity), svadhyaya (the study of sacred scriptures) and ishvarapranidhana (devotion to God). Tapas, contained in niyama, does not mean painful physical or mental penance, but the practice of conquering all physiological and psychological dualistic conditions (i.e., heat and cold, like and dislike, comfort and discomfort).

Prema (Preman) (Hindi: Prema)
Supreme love.
The highest and purest love, born of complete surrender and devotion to God. The ultimate form of love in bhakti yoga.

Purusha (Puruṣa)
The True Self; Atman.

Radha (Rādhā)
A lover of the Lord Krishna.

raja yoga (rāja-yoga)
Royal yoga.
The path of Yoga that leads to the realization of the True Master (True Self) by controlling prana (vital energy) and restraining the mind's activity through meditation.

raja yogi (rāja-yogin) (Hindi: rāja-yogī)
A yogi who practices the path of Yoga called raja yoga.

raga (rāga)
Greed.

Ramakrishna Paramahansa, Shri (Rāmakṛṣṇa Paramahaṃsa, Śrī)
(1836-1886)
A great enlightened being of modern India.
Shri Ramakrishna had a passion for God from his childhood and
was often absorbed in samadhi. At Dakshineshvar Temple in
the north of Kolkata (Calcutta), he had a vision of the goddess
Kali. He proceeded to practice all kinds of Yoga, and realize the
Truth of non-duality. He also realized the Truth of both Islam and
Christianity, and taught that all religions are but varying paths
toward one Truth.

Ramakrishna Mission
The monastery founded by Swami Vivekananda and his brother
disciples. The Ramakrishna Mission's goal is to spread the Truth
that Shri Ramakrishna taught: the eternal and imperishable Truth
of Oneness is in a diversity of religions.

Ramana Maharshi (Ramaṇa Maharṣi)
(1879-1950)
An enlightened being of modern day India who realized the True
Self through the experience of his own sudden death at seventeen
years of age, after which he abided permanently in Truth.

sadhana (sādhana)
One's training in Yoga, primarily the daily practice of asanas,
pranayama, and meditation.

sahasrara chakra (sahasrāra-cakra)
The chakra located on the crown of the head, represented as
a thousand petalled lotus flower.

sakhya (sakhya)
Friend.
One of the five bhakti attitudes toward God. In sakhya, the
bhakta interacts with God like an equal in a mutual relationship
of intimate friendship and everything is shared without condition,
including emotions.

samadhi (samādhi)
Complete absorption.
A state in which the mind is completely immersed in the object

of concentration, to the extent that it merges entirely with that object; the state in which one realizes the essence of one's object of concentration.

samana (samāna)
One of the five currents of prana (vital energy) in the human body. Samana works in the area between the heart and the navel, and governs the digestive function.
See "vayu."

sangha (saṃgha)
A gathering of practitioners or seekers of Truth; the company of disciples.

sanskara (saṃskāra)
Subconscious impression on the mind left by the various worldly experiences. Sanskaras later produce karmic consequences according to their nature and content.

Sat-Chit-Ananda (Sacchidānanda)
"Existence, Consciousness, and Supreme Bliss."
These words express the true nature of Brahman or True Reality.

satguru (sadguru)
See "guru."

Satori (Japanese transliteration)
Awakening or realization of the Truth.

satsangha (satsaṃgha)
A sacred gathering of practitioners who aspire to Enlightenment. The occasion where seekers assemble in the presence of an awakened being to receive his blessings and teachings.

sattva (sattva)
One of the three gunas (qualities), essentially characterized by lightness and comfort, with a tendency towards brightness.

sattvic
Characterized by sattva.
See above.

shakti (śakti)

The Goddess, as the divine energy sustaining the universe.
In the human body, shakti is considered as sexual energy and
is sometimes identified with Kundalini.

Shakyamuni (Śākyamuni)

"Shakya" is the name of a tribe from which the Buddha
descended. "Muni" means a saint or renunciate, especially
one who practices "mauna" or spiritual silence. "Shakyamuni"
(the saint of Shakya) indicates the Buddha.

shanta (śānta)

Peaceful.
One of the five bhakti attitudes toward God. In shanta,
the bhakta indulges in the bliss of God with a peaceful and
satisfied state of mind.

shanti (śānti)

Peace.

shri (śrī)

Honorific title.

sushumna (suṣumnā)

The most important nadi, located in the center of the spine.
Prana (vital energy) circulates through nadis and sustains
the body. The practice of Yoga purifies the sushumna and
awakens kundalini.

sukshma (sūkṣma)

Subtle or fine.
Distinguished from the gross physical body, the subtle body
is composed of intellect, ego, mind as an organ or function of
thinking or perceiving; five sense organs or capacities (hearing,
touching, seeing, tasting, smelling); five action capacities
(speaking, grasping, walking, excreting, procreating), and five
subtle elements (sound, contact, form, taste, smell). It is called
"sukshma sharira" (the subtle body) and becomes the substance
of reincarnations.

tapas (tapas)
Asceticism.
The internal heat generated by the struggle against egoism in the practice of Yoga. Tapas is also translated as "asceticism" since it represents pain for the ego.

udana (udāna)
One of the five currents of prana (vital energy) in the body. Udana presides over the ascension of energy from the nose to the crown of the head. It becomes active only when the physical body dies or in deep meditation.
See "vayu."

Universal Gospel of Yoga, The
A collection of selected essential teachings of Satguru Shri Mahayogi Paramahansa, delivered in satsanghas held in New York City between 1996 and 1998. This book contains practical wisdom for daily life and profound and timeless insight in plain, beautiful language.

Upanishads (Upaniṣad)
Indian scriptures, which reveal the secret wisdom, the Truth. Etymologically, the name indicates the esoteric teachings into which the master directly initiates the disciple who sits nearby. (Upa means near, ni-shad means sit down.)
The oldest Upanishads, collated in the period between 700 B.C.E. and A.D. 200, exposed the universal Truth that "Brahman (True Reality) and Atman (True Self) are one and the same; that is, the very essence of all things." For the first time in history, they revealed Yoga as the path to realize the Truth. Yoga today is a practical and experiential approach that includes the essence of the Upanishads' philosophy.

vatsalya (vātsalya)
Mother.
One of the five bhakti attitudes toward God. In vatsalya, the bhakta loves God as a mother loves her child.

vayu (vāyu)

Wind.

The converted form of prana (vital energy) manifested in the human body as five separate functions. Each "wind" presides over a specific function: prana, over the respiratory system; samana, over the digestive function; apana, over the excretory function; udana, over the ascension of energy to the crown of the head; and vyana, over the whole body.

Vedanta (Vedānta)

The final part, the ultimate (anta) of the Vedas, meaning the Upanishads; or, the expanded philosophy that developed subsequent to the teachings of the Upanishads. Vedanta philosophy declares Oneness as the True Reality of the universe (Brahman) and the True Self of all beings (Atman).

Vedas (Veda)

The oldest collection of sacred scriptures in India, which contains hymns to the gods and prayers recited during rituals. Veda means "wisdom." The words in the scriptures were worshiped as revelations of the gods brought forth by the direct inspiration of sages (rishis).

Vivekananda, Swami (Vivekānanda, Swāmī)
(1863–1902)

A great saint, Shri Ramakrishna's most beloved disciple, who brought the universal Truth of Yoga to the world. After the master passed away, Swami Vivekananda became a monk and, while wandering all over India, attained the Truth that the master taught him: "Everything is the manifestation of God himself." In order to save the suffering people he saw at that time, and to bring the universal Truth to the world, he took part in the 1893 Parliament of Religions in Chicago. His powerful gospel inspired and awakened many people to the Truth, regardless of nationality, race, or religion.

Vrindavan (Vṛndāvana) (Hindi: Vṛndāvan)

Location in India where the story of the divine love between Krishna and the gopis (cowherd girls) was born.

vyana (vyāna)

   One of the five currents of prana (vital energy) in the body.
   Vyana regulates the whole body, from the tip of the toes to the
   crown of the head.
   See "vayu."

Yogananda, Paramahansa (Yogānanda Paramahaṃsa)
(1893-1952)

   A saint of modern India who brought the universal Truth of
   Yoga to the West. After completing spiritual disciplines taught
   by his master, Shri Yukteshvara, Paramahansa Yogananda went
   to America in 1920 on the advice of a divine being, Babaji, to
   spread the gospel of Yoga. He taught pure love for God and the
   eternal and universal Truth. His intense devotion moved people to
   a great longing for God, beyond notions of East and West and the
   differences of religion.

Yoga Asanas

   Publication containing an introduction to yogic philosophy and
   teachings, and a detailed photographic guide to the practice of
   Yoga asanas.

yogi (yogin) (Hindi: yogī)

   One who has attained Yoga (Satori), or a practitioner of Yoga
   who is engaged in actual, continuous self-discipline to
   attain Satori.

Bibliography

Anandamali. Mahayogi Yoga Mission. *Pranava Sara*. Kyoto:
   Mahayogi Yoga Mission, 1999.

Brunton, Paul. *A Search in Secret India.* New York:
   E.P. Dutton & Co., 1934.

Gupta, Mahendranath. *The Gospel of Sri Ramakrishna*. Mylapore,
   Madras: Sri Ramakrishna Math, 1942.

Mahayogi Yoga Mission. *The Universal Gospel of Yoga:
   The Teachings of Sadguru Śrī Mahāyogī Paramahaṃsa.*
   New York: Mahayogi Yoga Mission, 2000.

Mahayogi Yoga Mission. *Yoga Asanas*. New York:
   Mahayogi Yoga Mission, 1999.

Venkataramiah, Sri Mungla. *Talks with Ramana Maharshi.*
   Tiruvannamalai: Sri Ramanaasrama, 1955.

Vivekananda, Swami. *The Complete Works of Swami
   Vivekananda.* 8 Volumes. Calcutta: Advaita Ashrama,
   1947.

Yogananda, Parmahansa. *Autobiography of a Yogi*. Los Angeles:
   Self-Realization Fellowship, 1946.

Mahayogi Ashrama (Kyoto)

May these invaluable teachings of Truth

Fill our whole existence, and

May our every breath, thought, deed,

Our everlasting gratitude and delight,

Be devoted to That,

Sweet Lotus Feet.

Mahayogi Yoga Mission Publications

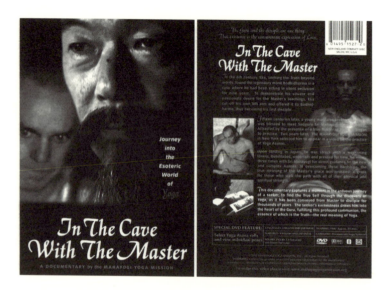

DVD: In The Cave With The Master

This documentary reveals the true essence of the ancient spiritual art of Yoga, which continues to exist in modern times. It provides a glimpse of the long and arduous journey of a disciple in his quest for spiritual Truth—a Reality known by few.

58 minutes. Region Free. 01495-1527-2

The Universal Gospel of Yoga

The Teachings of Sadguru Śrī Mahāyogī Paramahaṃsa

A collection of essential teachings from satsanghas that took place in New York City between 1996 and 1998. This book contains practical wisdom for daily life and profound and timeless insight in plain, beautiful language.

Art Paperback. 222 pp. ISBN: 0-9663555-1-2

MAHAYOGI YOGA MISSION

New York

228 Bleecker Street, #12
New York, NY 10014
www.mahayogiyogamission.org

Japan

258 Shimochojamachi
Onmaedori Kamigyo-ku
Kyoto 602-8361
www.mahayogi.org